TWAYNE'S WORLD AUTHORS SERIES

A Survey of the World's Literature

COLOMBIA

Luis Davila, Indiana University

EDITOR

José Asunción Silva

TWAS 505

José Asunción Silva

JOSÉ ASUNCIÓN SILVA

By BETTY TYREE OSIEK

Southern Illinois University

TWAYNE PUBLISHERS
A DIVISION OF G. K. HALL & CO., BOSTON

Printed on permanent/durable acid-free paper and bound
in the United States of America

First Printing

Library of Congress Cataloging in Publication Data

Osiek, Betty Tyree.
José Asunción Silva.

(Twayne's world authors series ; TWAS no. 505 : Colombia)
Bibliography: pp. 175–81
Includes index.
1. Silva, José Asunción, 1865–1896—Criticism
and interpretation.
PQ8179.S5Z78 1978   861   78-17211
ISBN O-8057-6346-5

Contents

About the Author

Betty Tyree Osiek is Associate Professor of Spanish in the Department of Foreign Languages and Literature at Southern Illinois University, Edwardsville, Illinois. She holds a B.A. degree from Lindenwood College, an M.A. and Ph.D. from Washington University at Saint Louis, Missouri. She has received the Jesse R. Barr Scholarship, the Max M. Bryant Fellowship and a Latin American Fellowship at Washington University while doing her doctoral work. She was awarded a postdoctoral Fellowship at the College Faculty Institute on the Problems and Development in Latin America, at Hamline University in Saint Paul, Minnesota. She has also taught at the University of Missouri in Saint Louis. Her publications include *José Asunción Silva: Estudio Estilístico de su Poesía* (México, 1968: Andrea). She is presently Vice-President of the Midwest Association of Latin American Studies. She is contributing editor for the "Poetry Section" of the *Handbook of Latin American Studies* published by the Library of Congress, and has given papers on Spanish American poetry and prose at regional, national and international conferences.

Preface

José Asunción Silva was an important late nineteenth-century literary figure, during the years when Hispanic-American literature was struggling to come of age. Silva was a Modernist who had very little effect on Spanish-American Modernism because his work was not published in any extension until 1908, after the peak of the epoch. Yet in retrospect, his work was an outstanding contribution to the Modernist epoch. In spite of his merit, little concerning him has been published in English. It is the aim of this study to demonstrate the value of his production.

This work is for the general public as well as for critics and students of Spanish-American literature. Its purpose is to give to those who might not otherwise know of Silva a basic background in his poetry and prose, and an understanding of his tragic life as related to his work. It also synthesizes the basic biographical and critical knowledge for those well versed in the subject. In the process of investigating his life and artistic achievements, I have examined the facts as objectively as possible.

Silva is one of the deceptively simple writers whose work is difficult to translate from the Spanish language because it is not easy to reproduce the rhythmic effect he displayed, especially in his poetry. No translation can do complete justice to his art. Nevertheless, I hope my translations will stimulate the reader who is not acquainted with Silva to read his works in the original, learning the language if necessary. The translations of poetry and prose citations are as literal as possible, and therefore do not attempt to produce the artistic effect of the original. Since no critical edition has yet been published, the texts used for citation were the least deficient publications of the works of Silva to be found.

The introductory chapter deals with the literary and historical background of Modernism and sketches the literary tendencies of that period. The chapter does not pretend to exhaust the material, but rather endeavors to pinpoint the main currents of the time.

It also presents a brief analysis of the configuration of Silva's particular type of Spanish-American Modernism, and of his Symbolist tendencies.

Chapter Two is biographical and attempts to present Silva's life as a process of development closely related to his work. At the same time, an underlying identity is sought in his reactions to the different tragic events of his life, and an attempt is made to establish the effects of that identity in his work.

Chapter Three is a study of his poetry in which an endeavor is made to elucidate the symbolic and thematic configurations governing his poems. Chapter Four considers at length *De Sobremesa* (After-Dinner Chat), in an effort to establish the relationship of this autobiographical novel to the author's life, and to analyze in depth the content, theme, and techniques. Chapter Five explores critically his brief prose works, with the exception of his letters to friends, family, and business associates. Silva's letters have been at least partially collected but, with the exception of two literary letters, they were excluded as being beyond the scope of this book. Chapter Six deliberates upon Silva's literary contributions to Spanish-American and world literature, and his influence upon those writers who followed him.

Acknowledgments

As is often necessary in an investigative work, many sources have been consulted and used. My thanks go out to every one of those students of the life and works of Silva. Without doubt, many debts of gratitude have been forgotten. The assistance of Dorlis Kirchner in the preparation of the manuscript has been invaluable, in both the mechanical part as well as the pruning of verbosity, since as Karl Marx said: "Time is needed to write short books," and time was limited. Professor Carlos Latorre is deserving of recognition for his assistance in reading the manuscript, offering suggestions for improvements in the translations into English, and questioning and clarifying various concepts. The editorial suggestions of Luis Dávila and Edward Longworth Spencer have helped immeasurably in polishing the language. Cynthia Mottin was a patient and long-suffering typist of the several "final" drafts of the manuscript. Joe Santee's counsel aided me in viewing the whole process more objectively. Acknowledgment is also due those students, both undergraduate and graduate, who served as a sounding board for many of the thoughts and ideas in the work. Appreciation also goes to Southern Illinois University at Edwardsville, where the opportunity was given to me to try out those concepts in classes on Spanish-American literature, and also for having granted me the time for the termination of this book. And last but not least, my gratitude goes to my husband, Edward Henry Osiek, source of strength and encouragement through fruitful as well as unfruitful days.

Chronology

1864   April 12: Assault upon ranch "Hatogrande," resulting in the murder of Silva's grandfather and severe injuries to his great-uncle.

1865   January 6: Ricardo Silva Fortoul is married to Vicenta Gomez Diago. November 26: Birth of José Asunción Silva in Bogotá, Colombia.

1872   Study in the school of Luis M. Cuervo.

1877   Goes to the school of Tomás Escobar.

1881   Has to leave school to work in his father's import store.

1882   December 16: Publishes version of Béranger's "Las Golondrinas" (The Swallows) in *Papel Periódico Ilustrado*.

1883   August 20: Publishes version of Guérin's "Fragment," which he entitles "Imitación" (Imitation) in *Papel Periódico Ilustrado*.

1884   April 29: Publishes the poem which begins "Encontrarás poesía . . ." (You will find poetry . . .) in *El Liberal*. Trip to Europe: Switzerland, France, and England. October 5: Death in Paris of Silva's great-uncle Antonio María Silva Fortoul, while Silva is en route to France.

1885   Civil war in Colombia causes economic ruin of Ricardo Silva Fortoul. July 24: Publishes a version of Hugo's poem "Realité," entitled "Realidad" (Reality), in *Papel Periódico Ilustrado*.

1886   Returns to Colombia from Europe. Publishes eight poems in an anthology of Colombian poetry entitled *La Lira Nueva* (The New Lyre). Publishes "Las Crisálidas" (The Cocoons) in *Parnaso Colombiano*, Vol. 1.

1887   February 15: Publishes "Taller Moderno" (Modern Studio) in *Papel Periódico Ilustrado*. June 1: Silva's father, Ricardo Silva Fortoul, dies in Bogotá: mourning at ranch "Hatogrande."

1888   August: Publishes letter of literary criticism to editor of *El Telegrama*, Sunday edition.

1890   December 14: Publishes "La Protesta de la Musa" (The Protest of the Muse) in *Revista Literaria*.

1891   January 6: Death of his sister Elvira Silva,, with another period of mourning at ranch "Hatogrande."

1892   November: Publishes "Los Maderos de San Juan" (The Wood of Saint John) in *Revista Literaria*.

1893   Publishes versions of five short stories by Anatole France and an introduction to the French writer and his works.

1894   Appointed Secretary of the Legation in Caracas, Venezuela. August 7: Publishes the famous "Nocturno" (Nocturne) in *Lectura para Todos* while in Cartagena, Colombia, on his voyage to Venezuela. October 1: Publishes "Anatole France" in *Cosmópolis* of Caracas, Venezuela. December 1: Publishes "El Doctor Rafael Núñez," in *El Cojo Ilustrado*.

1895   Return from Caracas, Venezuela. January 17: Sinking of the ship *L'Amerique* on the shores of Colombia, with the loss of his manuscripts. Resigns from diplomatic service. July 5: Recites at a diplomatic reception "Al Pie de la Estatua" (At the Foot of the Statue).

1896   May 23: Asks his friend, physician Juan Evangelista Manrique, to mark the precise location of his heart. May 24: Silva found dead by his own hand at the age of thirty years and six months.

CHAPTER 1

Nineteenth-Century
Spanish-American Literature

I Modernism

MODERNISM in Spanish America has had myriad inter-
preters who define it in several different ways. The many
diverse points of view deprive the term of a fixed or exact
meaning, although it is usually agreed that Modernism marks
the entrance of Spanish America into the mainstream of world
literature.

Following the lead of Federico de Onís, Modernism is now considered as an epoch rather than a "movement" or "school."[1] That
epoch is commonly judged to have manifested itself first in prose,
actually poems in prose, in writers such as Manuel Gutiérrez
Nájera and José Martí. Later these techniques appeared in poetry,
where they received more renown. Spanish-American Modernism
reached its peak in 1896, the date of Rubén Darío's *Prosas Profanas*,[2] and of the death of Silva. It began to decline by 1905,
lasting until around 1920.

The following tendencies are among those most commonly
listed in defining Modernism: 1) a self-conscious literary awareness of the poetic art and of the poet as a special kind of author
writing for personal, creative realization; 2) the effort to be
original, individualistic, and diverse in their art; 3) the idea of art
for art's sake, or of art as its own end, stimulated in part by the
lack of an appreciative public, which caused the writers' disillusionment, feelings of superiority, and such reactions as a desire
to escape from their culture; 4) a renewal of stylistic and artistic
preoccupations, with an emphasis on such qualities as intensity,
intangibility of themes, and musical treatment of them, while
demonstrating as well an effort to renovate form; 5) the evidence

13

of the influence of the Parnassians, and later the Symbolists, with some lingering Romanticism in tone and theme; 6) more frequent concentration on the exotic and cosmopolitan; and 7) an indication in many works of the profound spiritual crisis reflected in all aspects of life during the latter part of the nineteenth century, as manifested in libertarian, decadent, skeptical, pessimistic, and often atheistic or agnostic tendencies.

These distinctive features indicate that the main stress was on the aesthetic, but on a more profound level there was also an effort to comprehend the spiritual crisis of the period, to answer the metaphysical questions in a new and artistically pleasing way. The poets were reacting against Romanticism but at the same time were Romantic in some of their characteristics; for example, their desire to capture many shades of feelings and emotions, their rebellion, and their insistence on artistic liberty.

II Silva's Modernism

Some critics call Silva a figure of transition from Romanticism to Modernism, and a clear-cut division cannot be established between Romanticism and Modernism. Silva reflects, in some of his poems, such Parnassian tendencies as a striving for innovation as well as strong control of poetic form. There he concentrates, as did the Parnassians, upon embodying external perceptions in plastic and visual images.

Symbolic currents are also visible in Silva's poetry. He learned the Symbolist theories of the day in Paris, and felt a great affinity for them. He did not live long enough truly to master the Symbolist techniques, yet his poetry was Symbolic in that he wanted to reproduce, like Mallarmé, not the object, but the effect the object produces. Silva wanted to give a beautiful image of the imprecise, by the use of symbols, by correspondences between things, by transpositions from one art to another, and by synaesthesia or linking of the physical senses.

Silva struggled with the problem of language, with the possibility of expressing the ineffable. These were the preoccupations of the Symbolists, and Silva was in part a Symbolist although his symbols are not hermetic, nor are they easily observed in his restrained style, and for that reason many critics deny that he was a Symbolist. Yet in his best poems, such as the "Nocturno" (Nocturne), he creates a total symbol with a flowing, sinuous rhythm and musicality which is in close symbiosis with the symbol created. That rhythm and musicality also demonstrate the affinity of Silva with Verlaine's kind of French Symbolism.

From the Symbolists, Silva intuited the symmetry which must exist between thought and rhythm, between the symbol and the verse, successfully represented by the "Nocturno," which has given him great fame. There he succeeds in making the whole poem a single symbol and, through the enchantment lent by a rhythm invented solely for the content of that particular poem, attains a quintessential expression of human grief.

In contrast with the poetry of Ruben Darío, the Nicaraguan who is usually considered to be the principal poet of Modernism, Silva was a simple, natural Modernist in his poetry. Darío's work abounds in exquisite and consciously elaborated form, and ornate and decorative poems. These characteristics predominated in Darío's poetry, except in later years when he began to write poems in which he too meditated on life, death, and eternity. Yet Silva did use techniques similar to the earlier Modernist style of Darío in a parody he wrote of the "rubendariacos," the minor poets who were pedestrian imitators of Darío. Silva demonstrates his capacity to use Modernist techniques in this satiric poem, discussed in the chapter on poetry. However, with the exception of this ironic composition, Silva was a more simple Modernist in his poetry, more of a renovator of form, repudiating preciosity. Like the two Cubans José Martí and Julián del Casal, Silva employed more restrained language in his poems, but with musical and symbolical qualities, thereby adding beauty and profundity to his simple vocabulary.

In his prose, on the contrary, Silva reflects a mature Modernist expression which contrasts surprisingly with the attractive simplicity observed in his poetry. His essays use coloristic techniques, and the vocabulary he prefers is as ornate, elegant, and decorative as any of the other Modernists' production. His novel *De Sobremesa* (After-Dinner Chat),[3] is similar to the Modernist novel *Idolos Rotos* (Broken Idols),[4] by Manuel Díaz Rodríguez. In both there is an elaborately precious style as well as a comparable choice of subject. The two novels treat of the European experiences of an artistic aesthete who on returning to South America questions his ability to conform. While Díaz Rodríguez's hero is a sculptor, Silva elected to write in *De Sobremesa* the story of a neurasthenic poet who is presented as a psychological case study.

CHAPTER 2

Biography

I *Family Background*

ON November 26, 1865, the first-born child of Ricardo Silva Fortoul and Vincenta Gómez was born in Bogotá, Colombia.[1] Now a child had entered the home of the young couple to gladden their lives. Everything seemed rosy for the baby, who was born into a family which had moved in the social circles of the highest level for several generations. The Silvas were of Andalusian extraction and had migrated to Colombia sometime during the eighteenth century. Silva's mother, Vicenta Gómez Diago, of Andalusian and Navarran ancestry, was reputed to be an outstandingly beautiful woman. She and Ricardo Silva were married on January 6, 1865.[2] The Gómez family was originally from Andalusia and had been in Antioquia since the seventeenth century. Several of the men in the family had held political offices, such as councilman, in their native villages of Colombia.

Closer to Silva on his father's side, Antonio María, the poet's great-uncle, was a medical doctor, although he did not actively practice medicine; and Silva's grandfather was a businessman, owning a store replete with luxury items of many different types, such as silk of Jiriganor, editions of Elzevir, crystal of Murano, jewels of Lalique. His store was a kind of exhibition shop for articles too good for the moment, ahead of the times for a city as traditional as Santa Fe de Bogotá. The business served not as a vocation, but rather as an avocation, and the store was the family's social gathering center. The brothers had brought a ranch near Bogotá, called Hatogrande, from the estate of General Santander, and had finally returned to live there permanently in 1863.[3] The two Silva brothers were considered to be exotic in their tastes concerning clothing and other possessions, searching for the different and the unusual from high-fashion centers in Europe. This was contrary to the conservative tastes of the time, and to the practice in Bogotá of wearing the traditional dark clothing. Antonio María was considered to be somewhat eccentric and José Asunción was said to be a woman chaser, a good musician, an occasional gambler, as well as an "enamorado ferviente de la muerte" (fervent admirer of death). The last term suggests that this José Asunción, grandfather of the Modernist poet, was a daring and reckless person who did not fear confronting any sort of dangerous situation.

Each of the two brothers had one son. Ricardo, the poet's father, was the son of José Asunción, and Guillermo was the son of Antonio María. In 1860 Guillermo committed suicide because his father did not permit him to leave the ranch to celebrate Christmas Eve in Bogotá.

The ranch was the scene of yet another tragedy four years later when the brutal events occurred which caused Antonio María, the poet's great-uncle, to leave Colombia abruptly for Paris, never to return. A group of bandits, with the complicity of Jorge Gordillo, the man who did the milking for the family, attacked the ranch on the night of April 12, 1864. The group came down from the nearby hills, burst into the house, and spread out into the corridors and the rooms until they encountered the owners. Hatogrande was constructed in the form of a Latin cross, and each of the brothers had living quarters in one of the arms of the cross. Upon meeting Antonio María, the spokesman of the group of bandits told him that they were taking over the house. In the violent altercation which followed the brothers were beaten and stabbed repeatedly.

When they were found the next morning, José Asunción was dying, with sixteen wounds in his head. Antonio María was seriously wounded, not only in body, but in spirit. He was so shocked by the violent crime that as soon as he was well enough, he left Colombia permanently to live in Paris. And although there was a great deal of speculation about the real cause of the attack, two versions were most commonly given as the reason for the assault: a robbery, or a vendetta because of a woman.[4] The only person identified as one of the perpetrators was Jorge Gordillo. Whatever the cause, the crime and the accompanying gossip were ultimately to figure in Silva's attitude toward life and death.

These dramatic and tragic events, because they were discussed in later years, probably had a devastating effect upon the imaginative personality of the young poet, José Asunción. His great-uncle Antonio María departed immediately without getting the inheritance of his property settled legally. This complicated matters, since the court proceedings were more involved than normal, and his father, Ricardo had to enter into a lawsuit to try to straighten out his inheritance. The material loss to the family fortune forced Ricardo Silva to become an active businessman in order to earn a living for his family. These definite environmental influences cannot be ignored in the study of the development of Silva as a writer and as a person, for this tragedy was the beginning of the decline in the Silva family's fortune. Although without funds, his father had to take over and begin to operate the import store of luxury articles previously owned by Silva's grandfather. It was the only means of sustenance for himself and the bride he married six months later.[5]

Ricardo Silva, the poet's father, was thirty years of age at the birth of his son. He was described as a very handsome man, and was himself a writer of "artículos de costrumbres" (sketches about customs), which are traditionally witty and ironic and are still very provocative for the reader of the present. In 1859, when the father was twenty-three, one of these humorous sketches, "Un Domingo en Casa" (A Sunday at Home), appeared in a magazine, signed with initials R.S. The comical and witty article caused a flood of curious comments, as well as a rash of "cuadros de costumbres" (sketches about customs) in the same vein. In 1883, he published a book, which he dedicated to his son, José Asunción, containing this and all the other comical sketches he had written.[6] In spite of Ricardo's having published a book which was a well-known work in his time, the proud father admitted that his greatest work was his son.

Ricardo had fought on the side of the liberals in the campaign against the dictatorship of José María Melo in 1854, and had entered the capital with the winning Constitutional army on the fourth of December of 1854.[7] In spite of his father's liberal tendencies and inclinations, and those of his relative Santander, who had been president of the country, José Asunción was to be more conservative than liberal in his political beliefs.

On the day José Asunción was born, the response of his father indicates the kind of family into which he was born. The first action performed by his father after his birth was to go out into the patio and plant some eucalyptus trees. He was following the ancient proverb of writing a book, having a child, and planting a tree in order to claim having lived a full life. Such a deed by an erudite gentleman also shows us the intellectual and cultural level of refinement in Silva's home, where the expectations for the first-born son were certainly high. In his childhood, Silva remarked that the eucalyptus trees were the same age as he was, but that they would outlive him, reflecting perhaps not so much a pessimistic attitude as a knowledge, perhaps precocious, of the realities of human life and death and of the durability of nature.[8]

II   Atmosphere in Bogotá and in the Silva Home

The physical surroundings in Santa Fe de Bogotá in the epoch when Silva was a child, teen-ager, and young adult were not conducive to gaiety. The neighborhood where the family lived was one of the first parts of the city to be settled, and the houses were of colonial style. Unlike the tropical parts of Colombia, Bogotá has a rather chilly climate, making it difficult to live much social life in the streets, as often happens in the tropics. Therefore, since colonial times social life there has almost exclusively been limited to the social and literary gatherings of friends and acquaintances. Bogotá is 8,000 feet above sea level and is ringed by the higher mountains of the surrounding group of Andes, with the peak Monserrate bordering the city close to the neighborhood of the Silva family. Since it is cloudy a good part of the time, and it rains frequently, the city has a rather sad appearance. Naturally this does not mean that it makes everyone sad, but for persons inclined to be melancholy, Bogotá does not do anything to change that propensity. The mountains are for the most part not green, and that adds to the lugubriousness of the view, and the color impression given when the sun is not out is gray or grayish brown.

Many of the original houses of his neighborhood are still standing. Of course, they were not the huge houses which comfortably well-off people build today, but they were of good size and most had carved wood balconies or wrought-iron railings. The Silvas' house had an interior patio with the rooms arranged around it. This house, where Silva lived with his mother and sister in the period before his suicide, is now what is called a "casa de vecindad," or apartment house, with families living in each of the rooms of the house. There is a small plaque in front of the house which indicates that the Modernist poet lived here in the final days before his suicide. It reflects today a somewhat sad appearance. However, at the time Silva was alive, with all its luxurious furnishings, it must have been one of the most pleasing houses in Bogotá. The streets are narrow, and this too adds to the lack of light during the day, except when the sun shines brightly. The inside of the patio and of the house, like many colonial constructions, was filled with dark wood doors, door facings, and stair railings, and these too made the house somewhat dark, but when well cared for and well lighted, with the candelabra and chandeliers common in that time, these wooded areas would have reflected a polished patina that was not unpleasant.

The Silva family, at least nominally, had the ranch Hatogrande in their possession, and they went there for short stays, especially for their times of mourning. The house at Hatogrande was much larger than the one in the city. But it was a house which had belonged to General and later President Francisco Paula de Santander and was retained by the family. In his published letters Santander, a relative of the Silvas, mentions Hatogrande once, but it was more likely that it belonged to the government legally. (At present it serves as the summer house of the President of the Republic, and from that it can be surmised how large it was.) It has several acres of land which look quite fertile. When the Silva family had it there was room for raising some cattle and various crops. Located on the Sabana of Bogotá, it is an attractive spot with green and living foilage around it. But for the Silva family, it held sad and melancholy memories since it was the scene of the attack on Silva's grandfather and his great-uncle, and also the place where the family went to observe the rigorous periods of mourning which were observed in those days. Also, Hatogrande was the scene of inspiration for Silva's most famous poem, the "Nocturno" (Nocturne), written while recalling his deceased sister, Elvira.

In those days in Santa Fe de Bogotá, called by most, simply Bogotá, the influence of nineteenth-century Spain was still predominant in the literary and religious currents and culture of the capital of Colombia, high in the Andes. Life and society were gray and monotonous. But Silva's home was refined and unusual, filled with luxurious imported items, and thus from the beginning he felt contradictory influences emanating from a home on the one hand where all tastes were accepted, and on the other a traditional society such as was predominant in Bogotá at that time, a society which resisted anything new or innovative.

The Silva family home provided a popular meeting place for their friends and acquaintances. Many literary gatherings were held at the Silva home, and at those reunions the best productions in poetry and prose, of both novice and professional writers of the day, were read. Jorge Isaacs and Diego Fallón[9] were some of the more famous who attended. With such surroundings of exaggerated and refined luxury, as well as a high level of literary culture, in the conservative atmosphere of Bogotá, Silva and his family were the subjects of unfavorable commentaries, which often stemmed from envy.

Since his father was a writer, and Silva grew up in a literary atmosphere, it is not surprising that he should have dreamed of becoming a great poet. The literary group called "El Mosaico" with which Ricardo was connected included, among others, Manuel and Rafael Pombo, José María Vergara y Vergara, Jorge Isaacs, José Manuel Marroquín, Diego Fallón, and Salvador Comacho Roldán.[10] This group had their literary organ, *El Mosaico*, in which many of the humorous sketches of Silva's father as well as the other members were published. José Asunción witnessed their meetings, many of which were held in the Silva home. Early he must have learned one of the traits evident in his father's humorous sketches, the close observation of those around him. According to Baldomero Sanín Cano, Ricardo Silva was one of the leading writers of "artículos de costumbres" (sketches about customs) in their main period of popularity in Colombia.[11] One can see the qualities of a close observer and of a fine humorist possessed by the father in the prose and poetry of his son, José Asunción.

The family was well educated and several of Silva's paternal relatives were teachers, as for example, one old gentleman who at the age of eighty was still teaching Latin. On his mother's side, several of her ancestors were distinguished teachers of law or were practicing judges.[12] But the family had very few members who were successful in commercial ventures. Secretly it was murmured that Ricardo was successful at first in the import store because of his good luck and the aid of rich relatives. The import store was a popular place to go to buy luxury items and also a favorite gathering place of the dandies and writers. At first it seemed that the business was thriving under Ricardo Silva's direction, but actually his merchandising was based not on what would sell, but on what he preferred to sell. Thus, his business sense and his knowledge of good business techniques were weak. Alberto Miramón discusses how both father and son stocked beautiful articles which had no demand in Bogotá. They also unwisely imported articles from Europe, such as pianos, which cost so much when the shipping was included that they could not sell them for a profit.[13]

His father was an amusing observer of the realities and the preoccupations of his time. One still reads with a good deal of pleasure his "cuadros de costumbres" (sketches about customs), although they are somewhat dated, not only by the historical setting and the time they were written, but also by the witty, comical temperament of the writer. The influence of the family on Silva's works was strong, and one could say that these "cuadros de costumbres" were the basis of José Asunción's literary knowledge. He felt rather bitter about lacking a formal education and solid foundations for his knowledge.[14] Even though in large part self-taught, Silva knew French satisfactorily, spoke it correctly, wrote it with clarity and elegance, and translated it brilliantly. He also read in English and spoke it, although with some difficulty. All this education was gained by Silva through reading and studying in his free hours. Silva's bitterness at being self-educated can well be understood when one realizes, as his friend Baldomero Sanín Cano testifies, that his capacity to understand and his prodigious memory, which assimilated all that he read and heard, were both self-cultivated through his own reading and discussions with other writers and critics.[15]

Besides the literary atmosphere in the Silva household, José Asunción early in his life gained an appreciation for fine, luxurious clothing, furnishings, and decorations. His father, like his grandfather, had tastes that were unusual for conservative Bogotá. Their home had many imported articles of the latest European styles, as well as antiques of great value. In such a refined and literary atmosphere, the same variety of choice was available in books, and José Asunción had to be cautioned against his avid reading for fear of damaging his health.[16]

With such material advantages Silva never developed the Bohemian tendencies of some of his friends. He was raised to want beautiful possessions and therefore he was different from those writers who could live in poverty and perhaps produce better works of art because of it. Silva was not a writer who could suffer hunger. He was not a complete idealist. Because he was too proud to accept a life without material advantages, he escaped through suicide. This love of material possessions is reflected in his novel *De Sobremesa* (After-Dinner Chat).

III *Education, Personality, Tenor of Childhood*

It is not definitely known where Silva began his studies in primary school. Subsequently, he entered the school of Luis María Cuervo, a democratic establishment, with students from all social classes. Silva was unhappy there because of his incompatibility with his classmates, who gave him the nickname "el niño bonito" (pretty boy). He was soon moved to a more exculsive school headed by Tomás Escobar, but here also the name given him by the other students, "José Presunción" (José Stuck-up), reveals their resentment of his ability as a student, as well as his lack of modesty in the display of that ability.[17]

Why did the children dislike their classmate? First because of his unusual appearance for a schoolboy and the elegance of his possessions. But that was not the only reason. He always knew the right answer, making the other students in his class feel the desperation of never measuring up to his intelligence. His notebooks were always exceedingly neat, and his power of self-expression was undoubtedly superior since he had already written at least one poem at ten years of age. There was no false modesty in the child, and he had no inhibitions about expressing his knowledge, no matter what his classmates thought about the "curve-spiker."

In the words of his contemporary Daniel Arias Argáez, Silva's appearance at around twelve years of age caused the vehement envy of his classmates. He wore a suit of velvet cloth imported from Europe and made to measure, leather gloves always buttoned up, patent-leather slippers, bouffant silk ties, a silver watch hanging from a gold chain, and he possessed an ivory card case containing lithographed visiting cards that he would send to friends on birthdays and special occasions.[18]

The feelings of his classmates are understandable. Not only were they irritated by his elegance in the clothing he wore, his handsomeness, the correctness of his classwork, which reflected his near-genius level, but also by his superior use of the Spanish language. One can observe already the discrepancy between Silva and his surroundings.

Silva's personality reflected that discrepancy. An introvert by nature, he compensated for his lack of communication with others by displaying his superior ability as a student. However, the intensity of his desire to be like the very children whom he exasperated is revealed in an anecdote portraying his excessive behavior when advised by a friend of the family to stop acting like an adult and to indulge in more childish pastimes, like throwing stones at the pigeons. A short time later, José Asunción was observed on the roof getting ready to throw an eleven- or twelve-pound rock at the pigeons in the courtyard.[19] Nor did the poet at the age of ten resemble an ordinary child in his ability to express delicate emotions with such purity as in his poem "Primera Comunión" (First Holy Communion), where he speaks of "las voces ulteriores de otro mundo, sonoras y tranquilas . . ." (the far-away voices of another world, reverberating and tranquil).[20]

The fact that Silva was a genius and an artist does not mean that he did not have a nearly normal childhood. If Silva had been an only child one might understand why he had no experiences with other children and their games, but he was the eldest of six children, including Elvira, Julia, Alsonso, Inés, and Guillermo. The last three mentioned had died in infancy or early childhood.[21]

His avid reading, combined with his lucid intelligence, may well have given him a shorter childhood than many less well-endowed persons have, yet his poetry shows a nostalgia for this period of peace and innocence. The bitterness that is sensed in his poetry is most often concerned with the brevity, not the lack, of childhood. José Asunción was also familiar with childhood's pleasures as observed in the images of "Infancia" (Infancy), a poem which looks on childhood from a more mature period.

Con el vestido nuevo hecho jirones,	(With a still-new suit in ribbons
En las ramas gomosas del cerezo	In the gummy cherry branches,
El nido sorprender de copetones;	Surprise a nest of storks;
Escuchar de la abuela	Listen to grandmother
Las sencillas historias peregrinas;	With her simple, pilgrim stories;
Perseguir las errantes golondrinas	Chase the errant swallows;
Abandonar la escuela	Hurry away from school
Y organizar horrísona batalla	To rally a turbulent battle
En donde hacen las piedras de metralla	With cannonballs of stones
Y el ajado pañuelo de bandera.[22]	And a rumpled kerchief for a flag.)

As a child, Silva was inclined to be more serious than other children of his age. He was a good poet as early as ten years of age. Because of being precocious in his intelligence, he was accepted at an early age in the literary gatherings and was exposed to the best writers of Colombia of his time, and his father was one of his best literary friends. Naturally he seemed to be more of an adult than other boys his age.

In school he was not accepted by his companions except for those who were also superior and did not feel so threatened by him. It is not known what problems he had in the years just before his adolescence. But he showed a strange mixture of desiring to shock the bourgeois persons around him, and longing for acceptance.

He was an excellent observer of the persons around him and was an artist at ironically mimicking those who were amusing to him. Sanín Cano remarked that Silva had a surprising ability to imitate his friends and acquaintances and on citing their words he could produce their tone, their ideas and vocabulary.[23] This talent, of course, did not gain him many friends, and probably was one of the reasons that, in turn, he was informed of the parodies and jokes people made about him.

Perhaps until he was eighteen, when he traveled to Europe, he had the idea that his life might turn out to be normal, that he would someday marry and have a family. But with the kind of household setting he lived in, he must have felt even then that there was no girl beautiful or intelligent enough to interest him profoundly. Probably he did not feel the great lack of acceptance many young persons feel as they reach adolescence because of his acceptance at home and in the literary gatherings. Somehow his lack of approval by his classmates does not seem to have mattered so much to him.

IV *European Visit*

Silva was forced to leave the school headed by Escobar at the age of sixteen to help his father in his commercial labors. He was an avid reader and although he worked for his father during the day, he read and studied everything he could in the evenings, and also in his free moments in the import store of luxury items. Thus his energies had to go toward his process of self-education and his work in the store. For that reason he did not have the time to think much about his adolescence or to develop the adolescent complexes which sometimes result. Silva became an adult rapidly, and then the tragedies which followed did not permit him to return to that longed-for state of childhood.

His great-uncle, Antonio María, in the year 1884, invited Silva to come to Paris. After twenty years of separation from the family, he wished to provide his nephew a solid education in Europe. But Silva's bad luck seemed to follow his every step, and he did not receive the education his great-uncle had promised, since Antonio María died before Silva arrived.[24] A eulogy in

Papel Periódico Ilustrado gives the date of Antonio María's death as October 5, 1884.[25] Another account states that Silva had taken the trip to Europe, sent by his father in order to meet with their suppliers of goods for the store.[26] Whatever the reason for his trip, if Silva did participate in any formal university studies in Europe, it is not known. However, he was in Europe during the last months of 1884, and during at least part of 1885; in 1886 he was back in Bogotá.[27] He had visited in little more than a year London, Paris, and Switzerland. This trip was to awaken in Silva great aspirations which were difficult or impossible for him to realize with his limited financial means. He gained a lot from the trip because he had enriched his library with the books he bought, polished his social graces, and with his outstanding capacity for assimilation, had learned to judge the intellectual and literary movements of the moment in the countries he had visited. One can see that on his return he was even less able to adapt to the conservative society of Bogotá.

While in Europe Silva read everything he could find, attended lectures at the Sorbonne, and tried to learn everything he could, as was attested by Juan Evangelista Manrique. He met Silva in 1884 when he was studying medicine at the Sorbonne. Manrique says he spent some time with Silva during his stay in Paris, relating that Silva was interested in medicine and liked to talk to him about whatever medical texts he was studying at the particular time. He remarks that he wished to learn about the current literary situation in France from Silva. But he notes that Silva was often in strange and intransigent moods, reading widely and struggling to formulate an exclusive theory for all phenomena of nature. According to Manrique, he adopted the views of each of the writers he was reading at the moment. Manrique states that he advised Silva to accept the relativity of truth and try to get away from the idea of absolutes.[28]

These remarks by Manrique indicate to us that in spite of not being able to engage in formal university studies, Silva used his intelligence while in Europe to learn all he could about everything, even fields not connected with literature. And Silva probably gained much knowledge from a relatively short stay in Europe. Yet one can see it was without method and often with what might be called insufficient background, especially in the scientific fields. Only during his trip to Europe was he able to forget for a little while the fact that he would never be able to get a systematic education and also to forget that his father's store was immersed in financial difficulties. Perhaps neither he nor his father knew the extent of the deficit at that time.

V   *Return from Europe, Death of Ricardo, Religious Beliefs*

At first Silva was even more of a dreamer on his return from Europe than he had been before. But his dreams were to be short-lived. Until his return from Europe, Silva had not been given full responsibility for the business, and was more or less still an employee, even though when Silva was nineteen his father had gone to court to obtain permission for his minor son to become a full partner. He did not truly understand the financial predicament as his father did. And the financial problems were increasing by the moment, since in 1885 civil war in Colombia had caused the fluctuation of paper money, plunging everyone into economic troubles.[29] That civil war had resulted in an almost total cessation of internal and foreign commerce, and brought great harm to the business of Ricardo Silva.

In 1886 José stayed at the head of the business and his father went to Europe on a business trip. The latter had then been sick for quite a while, but had continued working. Shortly after returning from Europe, Ricardo died, on June 1, 1887, and when Silva became the legal head of the family import store, he discovered that his father had left him an inheritance of a business with a deficit of 44 percent.[30] Silva accepted the responsibility, although he could not have believed that it would ever be possible for him to recoup enough to pay all the debts. However, he felt honor-bound to clear his father's name if possible.

Silva probably felt obligated to clear his father's name because of pride in his family's social position. He was an idealist in his desire to keep the family name honorable. Not only was Silva himself proud of his social position, but so was the whole family, since they kept up with all social engagements, even during the time when the bankruptcy proceedings were going on, and when Silva was close to suicide. Probably the money for these gatherings came from Doña Vicenta, since she did not have to give up her own property, but why they did not change and live a more austere life under the circumstances can only be answered by the excessive pride they had in their position in society. They were unable to pay their debts, but were still trying to maintain the family's earlier social prominence without having the necessary wealth. The South American upper class then had a desperate need to maintain a front which did not reflect any financial change in their lives.

Miramón cites an anecdote by Sanín Cano which may shed some light on Silva's lack of knowledge of merchandising. In front of his import store there was a bazaar named Pórtico, owned by a Mr. Patiño, and once when Sanín Cano and Silva walked by this little store, Silva told Sanín Cano that he did not understand how the owner supported himself, nor could he understand how it could be a lucrative business to sell many items cheaply at so little profit per article. Silva told Sanín Cano that on the contrary he sold each of his articles at a high price, but the profit on each article gave him enough income to make several days carefree.[31]

After Silva's return from Europe his handsomeness was augmented by the new elegance of his clothing, purchased from the most famous tailors in Europe. With his silk ties, jackets with fancy designs, and fine batiste handkerchiefs, he had become even more of a dandy. He also brought back with him a considerable amount of knowledge about literature which, with his insatiable curiosity, he had learned in a short time because of his strong intellect and his talent for close observation. He also brought a collection of books which he proceeded to discuss with the writers among his acquaintances, spreading a knowledge of the new currents in European literature. But with all that he brought back, his surroundings in Bogotá began to stifle him more than ever, making him more sarcastic, and his dandy-like appearance caused half-hidden smiles, leering looks, and impertinent coughs. He was called without his knowledge "el casto José" (the chaste José) and "Silva Pendolphi." In countries where the obsession with manliness or "machismo" is strong, these types of insults are considered extremely cutting. Silva Pendolphi implies that he was an affected and effeminate poet,[32] striking at the same time at the lack of "machismo" in Silva.

Silva was raised in the Catholic beliefs of his family and they were indeed formative in his development. The influence of his religious education developed in him a preoccupation with morality, and a concentration on sin which is often visible in his anguished attitude concerning the erotic. This is especially visible in *De Sobremesa* (After-Dinner Chat). He drifted away from his religious faith, perhaps influenced by his reading and his study of many different agnostic and atheistic writers. Visible in his works is this ultimate lack of religious faith. At the deaths of Silva's father and of his sister, he had moments of renewed fervor, or else he was showing a kind of courtesy toward his loved ones. According to Arias Argáez, Silva had a spiritual crisis when he became a renewed practitioner of the Catholic religion after having left it for a long time. He says that at times Silva went to Mass with Guillermo Uribe. He was counseled by Guillermo Uribe, his main creditor, to read religious works and to return to the faith of his father, which gives one the idea that he had made it clear to many that his faith had suffered.[33]

In Silva's time in Colombia, if a person was not a Catholic, there was nothing else to be, and the person was looked upon as a complete religious outcast. And even though the person might suffer because of unfilled spiritual needs, there was little practice of other organized religions.

An anecdote told by Sanín Cano shows that Silva nevertheless did believe that the morality taught by the church was of some benefit. Sanín Cano, Silva, and some other friends were conversing near the cathedral one day when a man they knew removed his hat unctuously and went into the church. One of the young men said that there went a man who was a fanatic dominated by Catholic superstition. Silva replied that he did not dispute the designation but that it was the only human quality which remained, the only sincere sentiment, the only moral structure left to the man.[34]

VI   *Literary Activities, Bankruptcy, Family Relationships*

Although Silva showed his poetic inclination early, at ten years of age writing "Primera Comunión," his earliest artistic efforts were in art. Three of these early endeavors are known:

the first, a landscape at the age of three; the second, a calligraphic drawing of the Silva family tree at the age of thirteen; and the third, a charcoal reproduction of *The Duel,* by the English painter Samuel Edmund Waller. The latter was Silva's final effort in graphics, at the age of sixteen.[35] Though he would always be a fan of the graphic arts, José Asunción soon turned his creative energies more profitably toward writing, in which he demonstrated a superior talent.

Silva was writing during the years he worked for his father and after his father's death when the bankruptcy proceedings were going on. It would have been difficult for Silva to publish any of his poems at that time. He understood very well the effect it would have on some of the businessmen to whom he owed money, to know that their debtor was not struggling to repay them, but was occupying himself in artistic labors rather than devoting himself exclusively to the work of his store.

Three of Silva's translations or versions were published during hs lifetime: "Las Golondrinas" (The Swallows) by Pierre Jean de Béranger; "Imitación" (Imitation), by Maurice de Guerin; and "Realidad" (Reality), by Victor Hugo.[36] The only group of poems prepared by the poet for publication in a book during his lifetime appeared in *La Lira Nueva* (The New Lyre) in 1886, soon after his return to Bogotá from Europe. The eight poems by Silva published in an anthology of poetry by thirty-four young poets of Colombia were: "Estrofas" (Stanzas), later called "Ars" (Art); "Voz de Marcha" (Marching Song); "Estrellas Fijas" (Immovable Stars); "El Recluta" (The Draftee); "Resurrecciones" (Resurrections); "Obra Humana" (Human Work); "La Calavera" (The Roué); and "A Diego Fallón" (To Diego Fallón).[37]

He recited many of his "Gotas Amargas" (Bitter Potions) in the cultural gatherings where his friends learned them by memory and were able to gather them for publication later. Silva did not feel that ironic poetry was worthy of publication. Sanín Cano says that Silva did not intend to publish during his life any of the poems from "Gotas Amargas."[38] In addition, one of his essays, "La Protesta de la Musa" (The Protest of the Muse),[39] was written because of his feelings of disgust about satiric poetry and the following incident which happened in 1890.

A pamphlet was published by Francisco de Paula Carrasquilla, called *Retratos Instantáneos* (Instant Portraits), in which a great many people were savagely satirized in a manner in which they could tell who was being described. The pamphlet was a best-seller, selling out the afternoon it appeared. But in a few hours the people who were the subjects of the sketches went out armed into the streets of Bogotá looking for Carrasquilla. He had to escape from the country, guarded by a few of his friends to avoid bodily harm or murder. Then the press was deluged for a time with articles and poems against the burlesque poems from the pamphlet. The insults kept coming until one day Silva published his article of protest, mentioned above, against the flood of satire in both *Retratos Instantáneos* and in the newspapers, and, according to Arias Argáez, the irony and satire ceased.[40]

Another of Silva's lyrical prose pieces was written one day two years after Silva had been to the country house of Doña Rosa Ponce de Portocarrero, a well-known Colombian painter of her time. He wrote an open letter about their affection for art and its sacredness. This essay indicates Silva's ideas concerning the creative genius which provides for the writer and the painter a better world than that of ordinary humans.

While the ten-year period before Silva's death was the most productive for the Modernist author, less of his work was published during that time. In addition to the problems with his father's business, which was involved in some fifty-one lawsuits connected with the bankruptcy proceedings, several other tragic events occurred which caused the poet a great deal of suffering. The first of these was the death of his father in 1887,[41] which magnified the business dilemma, and then, the death of his beloved sister Elvira in 1891.[42] The bankruptcy was declared in that same year, but the debts owed to his fifty-one creditors, including his own grandmother, were not liquidated until 1893.[43]

Silva was deeply affected not only by the bankruptcy proceedings but also by the loss of his father. Then, at the death of his sister Elvira, he was thrown into a worse depression. Elvira, who was a girl of outstanding beauty and intelligence, was a sympathetic and understanding supporter of her brother in his artistic efforts. His sense of loss and bereavement was so strong that it resulted in one of the most beautiful poems concerning human grief ever to be written in the Spanish language. The poem, "Nocturno" (Nocturne), was published in 1894.[44] Previously Silva had written an elegiac poem, "Crisálidas" (Cocoons), inspired by the death of his sister Inés in early childhood. These poems will be discussed in Chapter Three.

The Colombian Romantic writer Jorge Isaacs paid tribute to Elvira in one of his best poems, which was 131 lines long.[45] Isaacs was of the same generation as Ricardo Silva. But he and José had a fast friendship because of the similarity in their lives. Both suffered bankruptcy because of their father's debts; both were unsuccessful and longed for their lost affluence the rest of their lives, always searching for schemes to regain that coveted position. Silva praised Isaacs's poetry highly, even going so far as to say that he was the only Colombian poet worthy to write an elegy about Elvira's death.[46]

Family ties were strong in the Silva family. In spite of these ties, Alberto Miramón says that Silva's mother, Doña Vicenta, was a practical woman who blamed many of her son's difficulties in making a living for the family on his eternal reading and writing.[47] This has been denied by the late Camilo de Brigard Silva, grandson of Doña Vicenta, who says that Miramón was wrong in his judgment.[48] He testifies that Doña Vicenta was one of the persons always most willing to support her son, and would have sacrificed her last cent to help him. He attests that she was a strong-willed woman and was able to accept the loss of her position in life, and that she handed over to her son all the money she had inherited from her mother and her husband without complaining. There is no evidence to prove that she did not bear all the problems well.

The tragedy of Silva and his sister Elvira did not end with her death nor with his. A poorly prepared edition of the poems of Silva gave Rufino Blanco Fambona the impetus he needed to postulate the theory that Silva and his sister were incestuous lovers. The critic theorized that "In short, it seems that they fell in love with each other. Was it solely the spiritual attraction of two exceptional persons? Did it go further? Did they love each other like Lucila and Chateaubriand? That a bond stronger than death existed between them is obvious; but was it blameworthy? Who can in such cases tell us, 'I know, I saw it'? All is induction."[49]

The badly prepared first edition of the poems of Silva[50] had grouped together three poems, as they had been in facsimile of the manuscript in Silva's handwriting, under the heading "Nocturnos." The first, which begins "A veces, cuando en alta noche tranquila . . ." (At times, late in tranquil night . . .), was amorous; the second, which begins "Poeta, di paso . . ." (Poet, say softly . . .), was erotic; but the third one, which begins "Una noche . . .") (One night . . .), contained no eroticism.

The first two amorous and erotic poems had been written at times different from the famous elegiac "Nocturno" and were not really connected with it, or with each other. However, the editors of the book assumed that the three poems were to form a thematic unity and printed just before the beginning of "Nocturno," which begins "Una noche . . ." (One night . . .), an unfortunate illustration of a young couple about to kiss each other. This illustration was the unfounded basis for Blanco Fombona's incestuous hypothesis. The second poem of the group of three exists in two separate versions, both in the handwriting of the poet, one called "Nocturno" and the other called "Ronda" (Night Watch). There were some minor textual modifications in the two versions. This indicates that the poet himself was not even sure of the title he wished to give the poem. Blanco Fombona admitted clearly that he was elaborating his own theory, and that there were no existing documents of proof. During Silva's lifetime, however, there had not been even a hint of such a relationship. When the legend was invented by the imaginative Venezuelan critic, as has been noted previously, several persons refuted such a hypothesis. For example, Emilio Cuervo Márquez testified that Rufino Blanco Fombona had never known either of the two, José or Elvira, nor had he gone to Bogotá to do any investigation of his allegation. He questions how the author could have dared to affirm that Silva felt a sinful love for his sister. He stresses his belief that the famous "Nocturno" shows nothing but a cry of abstract pain reflecting the tragedy of a brother whose beautiful sister, who was also his only confidante, had died.[51]

Many critics have followed the lead of Blanco Fombona and

have accepted the postulate of such an incestuous relationship. For example, the Argentine critic Alejandro C. Arias,[52] the French critic Max Daireaux,[53] the Spanish critic Ricardo Gullón,[54] and other writers of criticism and literary history too numerous to mention, have also followed the lead of Blanco Fombona. I would like to dispel that legend; however, as long as literary students do not have the full facts at their disposal, some will believe the account of the incestuous relationship, for bad news travels farther and faster.

Silva's friend Daniel Arias Argáez affirms the following concerning the legend of incest: "Concerning certain foul and absurd versions, which I have left completely destroyed several times, I do not want to bring them up again except to say that in honor of Colombia, such infamous legends did not arise in our environment but came from the outside, as certain epidemics which are less injurious than the unfounded slanders and unjustified defamation; fortunately, among us there are no people who are so evil that they would give rise to such infamous remarks."[55]

Alberto Miramón discloses that "Elvira Silva loved with all her heart—and this is important information to counteract clearly the incest legend—a cousin, Julio Villar Gómez."[56]

Alberto Miramón also cites the words of another friend of Elvira, Georgina Fletcher: "Silva, who loved beauty in all of its manifestations, could not be immune to the influence that his beautiful sister had over those who admired her. He [Silva] had enchanting dreams, also gloomy nightmares which his inspiration immortalized, but through the mind of this pure gentleman there could never have passed the idea that his verses might be interpreted with so much malice."[57]

Elvira died of pneumonia after having gone out on the balcony on the night of January 5 to view a comet. She was twenty-one years old. Silva's anguished sense of loss was all the more obvious since she had been one of his main sources of encouragement. Silva's reaction at her death was not one which most brothers would have displayed. He and Julio Villar entered the room where she lay dead, anointed her body with perfumed oils, and covered her with flowers.[58] But, given the poet's appreciation of not only his sister's personality, but of her beauty, his reaction was really that of the sensitive aesthete that he was, somehow to preserve as long as possible in his memory her corporal beauty.

Silva cultivated his love for his lost sister assiduously after her death and always had with him a photograph of her. He spoke of her with anyone who remembered her, as for example he does in a letter he wrote to Doña Vicenta from Caracas about the possibility of visiting the titular president of Colombia, Dr. Rafael Nuñez: "I will write you in the next letter telling you about my visit with Dr. Nuñez. She [his wife] is a fervent admirer of Elvira's beauty; she has a photograph, and she has sent me a message that when I come to see her I should bring her the one I have."[59]

VII *Love Interests*

In connection with the idea of Silva's incestuous passion for Elvira, it is important to consider what kind of love life the poet had. No letters or proof of the existence of love affairs have been found. But several of his contemporaries, including Baldomero Sanín Cano, have said that he was a gay young blade, and that he had more than one feminine acquaintance to whom he directed his attentions, but not with serious intentions. It has been disclosed that he kept an apartment, or "garconniere," where he entertained his female friends. Arias Argáez attests that "José Asunción, who was never a misogynist, was fond of flirtatious adventures. Naturally, gentleman and artist, he acted discreetly to protect his adventures from morbid curiosity. But a fortuitous incident lifted the veil of secrecy. There was a fire, that fortunately had no worse consequences, in a house on 19th Street, a few steps below where today the statue of Don Miguel Antonio Caro has been raised. The police came and logically the neighbors came also. In order to expedite the rescue operations, it was necessary to force open the door of the contiguous premises. There the surprised eyes found soft divans, rich carpets, refined works of art, pictures of girls with passionate inscriptions. . . . It was the love apartment of José Asunción."[60]

Silva died a bachelor, and although it is undoubtedly untrue to say that he died without experiencing sexual love, his poems indicate that he rejected the ties of a love affair that was unworthy of him, and he knew that because of not having success in business, he could not think of ever marrying.

Some of his friends and acquaintances have said that he was sexually timid, and as was mentioned he was called in Bogotá "el casto José" and in Caracas "La casa Susana" (Chaste Susana). The latter term, coupled with Silva's super-refinement for a male, caused the supposition that he was homosexual to be circulated among the high society of Caracas. Carlos García Prada opines concerning the origin and veracity of the legend: "In the Venezuelan capital Silva soon turned into the best intellectual stimulant of the young men who edited the magazine *Cosmópolis*. They respected and admired him. On the other hand, the 'Caraqueños' of high society, 'secretly and without harmful intent,' says Pedro César Dominici, called him 'Chaste Susana,' 'in spite of his masculine voice, which in no way recalled the honest woman of the biblical episode.' It was natural. . . . To those Don Juans of the tropics, Silva seemed effeminate. He did not accompany them in their licentious adventures. He did not appreciate either the easy, or the cheap, or the vulgar."[61]

It was also said that the women who knew Silva believed him to be a somewhat effeminate man, not the very masculine "macho" type which was the prevalent ideal of masculinity. According to Daniel Arias Argáez, the only woman Silva truly loved rejected Silva and looked for an unlettered, but forcibly masculine, husband to be her marriage partner.[62]

These contradictions in the interpretation of what Silva's love life was like may be resolved perhaps by looking at his works. They reflect that, like the majority of men, his sexual instincts were aroused and became active at puberty or shortly thereafter. As Miramón has said, in Silva's first poems the sense of the erotic is visible with romantic configurations; afterwards his adolescent attitude develops in a more sentimental, melancholy manner. Then as he becomes more mature, these sentimental feelings are destroyed by reality and the female becomes solely the object of his sexual desires.[63] But he was irritated by this latter concept and, in several of his poems of "Gotas Amargas" (Bitter Potions), he shows a clearly visible scorn toward the flesh, or a desolation at the lack of depth in these carnal encounters, finally resulting in an aversion toward physical love that perhaps would have diminished had he been able to think of marrying and establishing a family. But his tragic life with all the financial problems had prevented him from even considering the possibility of taking on the added burden of a wife. In his novel, *De Sobremesa* (After-Dinner Chat), there is the frustrating search of the protagonist, often considered to be Silva's alter ago, for an ideal of innocent womanhood, a girl whom he wishes to marry. He finds instead on all sides easily seduced women, reflecting in his protagonist the same feelings Silva demonstrates in many of his poems.

But in the famous "Nocturno" none of these carnal ideas is visible, and it is interesting to think about how Silva was inspired to write the poem. After the death of Elvira, as was the practice, José, together with his mother and his sister Julia, went to Hatogrande to spend the customary time of mourning. There, in gloomy solitude, Silva conceived the "Nocturno" while walking alone on the high plateau called the "Sabana of Bogotá." Here he and Elvira had walked together before her death. This memory was especially poignant for Silva, since the last time they had walked there together was during the period of mourning for their father.[64]

VIII   *Loss of Financial Backing*

Silva indicates some of his feelings at the time of Elvira's death in the superabundant 101-page letter he wrote to Guillermo Uribe, businessman and personal friend of Ricardo Silva and the principal financier of the Silva firm. In that often bitter and ironic letter, he explains to Guillermo Uribe his actions. He says that on January 6 Elvira became ill, and he remained with her and the family until her funeral on January 11. Afterwards, in a long explanation, he says that he became ill and was prostrated by grief, unable to do anything or even think. The reason for this long explanation is that Silva, in addition to his father, had also borrowed from Uribe for personal expenses, among other things for the expense of Elvira's funeral. He was thus explaining why he had not repaid at least the personal loan.

He had tried to borrow enough from Uribe to recoup the business losses inherited from his father, but Uribe had refused to lend him any money on the business until the debts owed by the father were repaid. Uribe insisted on the repayment of all the loans, including the debt inherited by Silva from his father. He insisted that the repayment of his debts had priority.

The length of the letter from Silva to Uribe seems excessive, and perhaps for this reason the letter has not been reproduced. Silva's nephew, Camilo de Brigard Silva, cites from it in two articles.[65] However long the letter may seem, it is a reply to Uribe's attack on Silva for not repaying his debts. Silva answers his accusation that he had taken the dishonest action of hiding away property, and discusses Uribe's threat to bring a criminal suit against Silva. The letter shows Silva's disappointment in the treatment he received from this old friend of the family[66] who was one of the principal agents in his economic destruction.

According to the law of the time, the creditors had to agree among themselves, and the person filing bankruptcy was forbidden to make any arrangement individually with the persons he owed. The proceedings took a long time because the creditors could not agree among themselves. They had followed the advice of Guillermo Uribe, and each creditor had taken his or her claim to court. Uribe had given that advice because he knew that if they did as he suggested the debt owed him would take first priority.

The law dictated that debtors who had public documents were in a privileged position with prior rights to repayment. Private agreements were secondary in priority. Within these two priority rankings, the debts were to be paid in chronological order according to the respective dates of the agreement.

This law probably was the main instrument in causing the complete financial ruin of Silva. Guillermo Uribe, who had a public document, had the largest amount owed him and he was not willing to take 80 percent of his debt, but rather wanted all his money first. Thus Silva could not terminate the seemingly endless bankruptcy proceedings and was not permitted to search for or take any kind of position until all the process had been completed.

Uribe did not want to help Silva, and although he had been a longtime friend and business associate of his father he developed a violent antipathy toward the son of his old friend, and actually tried to harm him as much as he could. Not only did he use his influence to keep the debtors from agreement among themselves, but he was one of the first to notify the banks in Bogotá of Silva's likelihood of going broke, causing them to deny him the possibility of borrowing funds from them.[67]

Silva had turned over to the Bank of Colombia all his stock of merchandise, credits, money, and personal property, or at least a good part of it, as he attests in the long letter to Uribe, except for the furniture of the house and his mother's jewelry. Silva offered his mother's jewels upon her insistence, but they were not accepted. Even though Silva had to relinquish most of his personal property, he probably kept most of his library.[68]

It has always seemed somewhat strange to the author that the property Hatogrande was not mentioned in the letters as one of the assets sold to enable the Silva family to repay some of the debtors in Silva's bankruptcy proceedings. It apparently remained in the hands of the Silva family, since they spent some time there in mourning the death of Elvira. It is now the summer house of the President of Colombia, and probably at the time of Silva's bankruptcy it belonged, at least in part, to the government.

With no possibility of obtaining a job until the bankruptcy proceedings were terminated, Silva poured out his melancholy and bitterness in his poetry, and began to work on a series of short stories he hoped to publish sometime in several volumes, to be entitled *Cuentos Negros* (Dark Tales), and on the volume of poems he intended to give the title *El Libro de Versos* (Book of Poems).[69] Silva also continued to work on his long autobiographical novel, *De Sobremesa* (After-Dinner Chat), 1887–1896.

IX *Diplomatic Service, Shipwreck of the* L'Amerique

During these final years of his life before his suicide, Silva must have felt desperate. When the bankruptcy proceedings were finally settled and he had the freedom to search for a job to support his mother and sister Julia, his mother used her influence with an old friend of the family, President Miguel Antonio Caro, to obtain for her son a diplomatic post. Although Silva was not a favorite of Caro, because of his long friendship with the Silva family Caro signed in 1894 the appointment of Silva as Secretary of the Colombia Legation in Caracas.[70]

After arriving in Caracas, Silva went for an audience with the titular president, poet Rafael Núñez. Núñez had stepped down leaving Caro in power, and had quite a bit of influence over Caro. They had several interviews, and Silva indicated in his letters to his mother that he felt Núñez was his friend and supporter. However, Núñez died during that same year, leaving Silva with only the half-hearted support of Caro. Nevertheless, Silva did publish that same year an article of literary criticism that he had written about Núñez.[71]

In the letters which Silva wrote to his family and friends from Caracas he showed a vivacious appreciation of his acceptance and high acclaim in Caracas upon his arrival, when very few persons in Bogotá would have given him such recognition. During this period Silva did manage to publish a few other translations as well: versions of five short stories translated from *L'etui de Nacre* and *Balthaazr*, by Anatole France, preceded by a biographical and critical article about the French author.[72] Finally, during his time in the diplomatic service, the famous elegaic "Nocturno" was published for the first time in Cartagena, Colombia, in *Lectura para Todos*,[73] causing a lot of excitement in literary circles.

When this "Nocturno" was published, Silva was being received with adulation in Caracas, especially by the younger writers, many of whom admired and respected him. Silva found himself widely appreciated and applauded for his literary work as he had never been in Colombia. For that reason, although not publishing much, Silva wrote more and seemed to be in better spirits. In his letters he mentioned his current literary activities. In addition to articles of literary criticism, he continued to work on *De Sobremesa*, "Los Poemas de la Carne" (Poems of the Flesh), and a series of sonnets he intended to call "Las Almas Muertas" (Dead Souls), which he referred to as his jewels. He worked on several other poems as well.[74]

Almost from the very beginning Silva did not have good relations with the head of the legation, a General Villa. In a letter to his mother and sister he used the derogatory term "patrón," which means "big boss," instead of "His Excellency the Minister."[75] In 1895, at the death of Núñez, virtually his only real supporter in the government, Silva requested a leave and then he started back to Colombia. En route, the ship in which he was traveling, *L'Amerique*, found herself in a severe storm which lasted three days and was finally driven onto the rocky Colombian shores.

The ship *L'Amerique* had made good time from Caracas, but on reaching the shores of Colombia she was damaged and began to sink. Two lifeboats were launched, but both sank because the water was so rough. The waves were so strong and high that no help could come from the shore. The passengers were there for three days, and then in the terrible moment when the ship was going down, about seventy of the people on the boat got into the heaviest of the lifeboats and were able to make it to shore. They had to cover up the boat with sails to keep the water from entering the boat and sinking it. They arrived safely at the port and all were saved, including Silva and another writer, a Guatemalan writer of chronicles, Enrique Gómez Carillo. These two Modernists did not become friends during this mishap. Silva thought Gómez Carillo was going too far in his stoicism when he read during most of the three-day ordeal. On the other hand, Gómez Carillo did not appreciate Silva's anguished, spectral attitude upon losing a good part of his manuscripts. All the passengers in the boat were lucky to escape with their lives, but Silva was greatly affected by the loss of the bulk of the unpublished manuscripts from his earlier period of productivity, and what he had added to them during his stay in Venezuela. Naturally, this was a deadly blow to the poet, making him feel that life held only disappointment and defeats for him.[76]

X *Final Efforts to Earn a Living, Final Literary Production*

Although depressed and demoralized, on arriving in Bogotá Silva tried to undertake his responsibilities as head of the family. During his time in Caracas, Silva had tried to think of a way to make a living for his family which would pay better than the diplomatic service. He had observed tile and cement factories in Caracas which seemed to be very successful, and he returned with the idea of establishing such a business in Bogotá. But he was unable to inspire the confidence necessary for borrowing enough money to succeed. Also, he did not know how to start in a small way, and antagonized his backers by the luxury of his private office even before getting the factory built. He was a dreamer, but at the same time his ideas were not completely without basis, since the business which he wished to initiate in Bogotá did later on have remarkable success. After his first burst of optimism concerning the success of the factory had subsided, Silva soon despaired and relapsed into a state of pessimism. Once again Silva had to turn to the idea of a diplomatic assignment, but on seeking a reassignment, he was offered the position of Business Attaché in the Nicaraguan Legation. The salary was so meager that he could not accept.[77]

A year before his death, Silva recited "Al Pie de la Estatua" (At the Foot of the Statue) at a reception given by the Minister of Venezuela.[78] Even in the only epic poem written by Silva, one about the hero Bolívar, the poet reflects his own melancholy and pessimistic attitude which had now engulfed him completely. (See Chapter Three for a fuller discussion of this poem by Silva.)

Silva felt himself incapable, as can well be understood, of the task of rewriting all of his works lost in the shipwreck. One of his friends, Hernando Villa, who feared that Silva might be contemplating suicide, urged him to reconstruct some of the works lost in the ship L'Amerique. José told him that he lacked the energy and desire to rewrite all of them, but that he would rewrite one, whichever one he preferred. Villa chose De Sobremesa, and because of his choice, his autobiographical novel is the only long prose work of Silva available today.[79] But Silva was now thoroughly disillusioned and was preoccupied with death, as his later verses show, as in the poem dedicated to Bolívar.

Twelve years after Silva's death, the few poems known to have been published during his life, plus fifty-odd other poems he wrote which had not been lost in the shipwreck, were published.[80] Those which had been copied down or memorized by friends were also published in subsequent publications. In later editions his critical articles and other short prose essays were collected from the periodicals where they had appeared. In several editions, selections are included from his novel De Sobremesa, selections which were often given titles by the editors of the publications and published separately as short prose essays before, as well as after, the manuscript of the novel was published in its entirety.[81] In 1925 *De Sobremesa* was published in its first edition, and later formed a part of the collections of his complete works.[82]

Silva was not well known in Colombia during his lifetime, except to those who had listened to his poems. Many of the poems he recited were the ironic and bitter poems called "Gotas Amargas" (Bitter Potions). Silva probably recited them for their shock value, or as a way of compensating for the lack of understanding of his poems, since it was generally known that he did not believe that ironic poems were worthy and did not intend to publish any of his "Gotas Amargas."[83]

Upon his death he did not become an immediate success, nor indeed was his true stature recognized for many years. Often his best poems, like the famous "Nocturno," were satirized mercilessly, during his life as well as after his death. One such example is the novel *Pax: Novela de Costumbres Latinoamericanas* (Peace: Novel of Latin-American Customs), which was published by the Imprenta de la Luz in Bogotá in 1907 and was written by Lorenzo Marroquín with the collaboration of José María Rivas Groot. One of the important characters of the book was S. C. Mata, who was said to be a caricature of José Asunción Silva. Within the book there is a parody of the famous elegiac "Nocturno," ridiculing the sublime expression of Silva.[84] And his works have not had very good luck in being published in high-quality editions which respect the author's own text. Also, as has been observed with the illustration printed in the first edition, even the editors did not understand his poems.

XI *Suicide*

Silva's suicide was premeditated, since he visited his friend the medical doctor Juan Evangelista Manrique on May 23, 1896, and after an offhanded question about his dandruff and incipient baldness asked if it was true that through percussion the doctor could determine the form of his patient's heart. Manrique marked the outline of Silva's heart on his chest and put a mark on the lowest portion.[85] Silva went home and took part in a social gathering planned by Doña Vicenta and her daughter Julia at around nine in the evening.

It seems strange that the family had a social gathering on the night before Silva committed suicide. His life was surely grinding down to a halt, because of lack of financial possibilities. Yet his mother and sister seemed to be going on with the same type of social gatherings they had always had. This would seem to reflect a great deal of pride of social position by the Silva family, and a lack of communication among Silva and his mother and sister about his own absolute inability to accept the poverty which was going to come to them. They too, although probably they could have accepted poverty more easily than José Asunción, were unable to think about living in a way different from that in which they had always lived.

That evening José did not show any less animation than on other occasions; he was as witty and festive as usual in such gatherings. The guests left after eleven.[86] Sometime during the early morning hours of May 24 he pointed at the target marked by Manrique and shot himself with the gun he had asked his mother to give him the day before on some pretext. The body was not found until breakfast time. Before he killed himself, Silva had smoked several cigarettes, waiting until everyone was asleep, and the shot was not heard.[87] This desperate poet deliberately took his own life rather than continue to hope for uncertain future happiness or resign himself to his somber existence with his pride destroyed.

Doctor Juan Evangelista Manrique, who had known Silva for at least ten years, put the mark on Silva's chest even though he must have been aware of the financial problems, and of the tragedies in Silva's life. Surely he must have thought that Silva might have some ulterior motive in asking him to mark on his chest the outline of his heart. Perhaps he thought it was just another aspect of Silva's insatiable interest in medical subjects which Silva had displayed in Paris twelve years before when Juan was studying medicine there. Silva had been heard to make the remark, "A mi verán primero muerto que pálido"[88] (they will see me dead first before seeing me turn pale), but perhaps the strength of these feelings was not visible to those closest to him.

On the night stand near his bed were found two books, *El Triunfo de la Muerte* (The Triumph of Death) by Gabriele

D'Annunzio, and one by Maurice Barrés in which appeared a section entitled "Tres Estaciones de la Psicoterapia" (Three Stations of Psychotherapy), and a copy of the English trilingual magazine *Cosmópolis,* in which there was an article dealing with the artistic technique of Leonardo da Vinci. According to Ricardo Riaño Jauma, Silva was planning to write an article on the Florentine painter and sculptor.[89] Some critics have advanced the theory that the D'Annunzio novel might have had something to do with Silva's decision to commit suicide.

It is not difficult to find many reasons for his suicide—his financial problems, business failures, the death of his father and then of his beloved sister Elvira, the loss of his diplomatic job, the loss of his works in the shipwreck of the ship *L'Amerique,* the lack of acceptance of his works in his native country as compared with his acceptance in Venezuela. All of these reasons can be considered as part of his decision to commit suicide. The tragic news of Silva's death at the age of thirty years and six months spread rapidly through Bogotá, and one of the city's leading newspapers published a cryptic note reflecting either the lack of knowledge of his talent, or the dislike of Silva by many of his contemporaries: "Young José Asunción Silva killed himself. It seems he wrote verse."[90]

Guillermo Valencia points out that Silva's coat of arms read "Nada de Nada" (Nothing from Nothing).[91] Perhaps this indicates that he was a nihilist, but more likely it was a way of stating his lack of optimism in a life where nothing ever turned out well for him.

Miramón relates an incident told to him by Baldomero Sanín Cano which reflects Silva's idea that suicide always seemed to him to be a natural and logical action. The two friends were crossing the street one afternoon in 1896 when a woman committed suicide before their eyes by throwing herself from a high balcony. Sanín Cano was so upset that he felt he was going to be sick, but Silva did not lose his serenity. Silva said to Sanín Cano, "Why such distress? Not only does she have a legitimate right to kill herself, but she did the best thing she could have done. She was ill, 'Brake,' a poor deluded woman who believed she was being followed, spied upon, hated by an infinite number of persons, and she would not have delayed long in becoming the persecutor. A person like that, as you understand, is not only useless but dangerous to society."[92]

Silva was buried in the suicide cemetery near the city dump. Some thirty-eight years later he was moved to the family pantheon and placed beside his sister Elvira.[93]

When the poet's accounts were examined after his death, it was found that the last check he had written had gone to a florist for a bunch of flowers for "la Chula," the nickname he used for his youngest sister, Julia. The amount represented, except for a small amount of currency, the whole capital that Silva possessed on the day of his death.[94]

In conclusion, the tragic life of Silva shows that his experiences could never be considered happy after his childhood. And yet his work is in a way a result of this tragic biography, and it explains and illuminates even more clearly the reasons for some of his themes, and for the very existence of some of his works. This poet of human grief created art from his tragedy, unlike those who experience tragedy in life but are incapable of creating art from it. The result is that the themes of his poems and prose which preoccupied him most throughout his lifetime were connected with his own feelings of personal disillusionment and despair: human solitude, the impermanence of human life and its fleeting pleasures, the endurance of nature, and the vanity and emptiness of existence.

CHAPTER 3

Poetry

I Editions of Silva's Poetry

THE different editions of Silva's poetry[1] contain varying numbers of compositions, from forty-five in the first edition[2] to eighty-five in the most recent.[3] From the beginning, the work of Silva has been mutilated.[4] The editors made changes in the texts of his poems, and they chose their own titles for some he left untitled or was unable to choose which of two he preferred. They published what were called his complete poems without knowing that several were scattered in recondite periodicals, and in the memories of persons who had seen them or heard them. He had given a notebook of adolescent poems to friends who made a duplicate copy, and this copy has recently appeared.[5] Some poems have been attributed erroneously to Silva, and the authorship of others has not been definitely proved. He himself mentioned poems he had written which have never been found. The editors of the earliest editions suppressed the sarcastic poems, "Gotas Amargas" (Bitter Potions), that Silva had preferred not to have published. For that reason they were not included in the manuscript he prepared, but after his death they were reconstructed from the memories of friends.

Silva left among his papers the following: the manuscripts of *El Libro de Versos* (The Book of Verses),[6] and his novel, *De Sobremesa* (After-Dinner Chat);[7] some loose leafs of plans for works he was thinking of writing; a sonnet and two stanzas of another with the title "Sonetos Negros" (Black Sonnets); the first version, on letter paper, of the "Nocturno" (Nocturne), which begins "Poeta, di paso . . ." (Poet, say softly . . .), entitled in the poet's handwriting: "Ronda" (Night Watch). But during Silva's lifetime, only thirteen poems and three versions of translations were published in anthologies and in periodicals.[8]

49

The first edition of the verses of Silva in book form was not a good one for several reasons. The editors tampered with the text and presented undocumented and incorrect biographical and critical information. The illustrations chosen were unfortunate, especially the one misrepresenting the emotions of the elegiac poem dedicated to Elvira.

The same editorial house, Maucci, published a second, augmented edition in 1910, another in 1918, and the last one was probably published late in 1918.[9] Although said to be augmented, the addition of a few poems did not improve the quality of the publication.

In 1923, Baldomero Sanín Cano prepared for publication in Paris a more complete and improved edition for which he had written the notes. The prologue by Unamuno was also reproduced. The volume included a section of the "Gotas Amargas" at the end. This edition served as the text of the poems published in later editions.[10]

Edition has followed edition with many of the same errors reprinted in the texts of the poems. Some have followed the index of the facsimile edition using the title *El Libro de Versos,* but usually adding some sections.[11] The three Aguilar editions were the most authoritative as far as the texts of the poems are concerned, especially the 1963 edition,[12] until the publication of the popular edition of the *Poesías* (Poems), edited by Hector Orjuela,[13] where he includes the unknown and forgotten poems by Silva, discovered by several investigators. Professor Orjuela indicates that he followed the texts of the poems found in the edition by the Banco de la República of Bogotá[14] but it too has some lacunae and textual modifications.

Poems and articles are still being found and, little by little, the complete works of Silva are being collected. Often these poems present difficulties in determining if they are truly Silva's, even when his name is given as the author .In most cases, these are the least important of Silva's work, but in the interests of scholarly completeness they need to be collected. A recent article documents the discovery of yet another unknown poem by Silva, and gives some information concerning the mysterious little notebook of his adolescent poems.[15]

Because of problems of dating many of the poems of Silva, a

thematic approach is more profitable than a chronological, developmental one. However, one can divide his work into two periods: one lasting through his adolescence until his return from Europe, 1875–1885, and the other from his return until his death, 1886–1896. One can then determine roughly into which period the majority of his poems fall. Some critics have said that Silva's adolescent production included occasional poems without importance and should not be considered as the essential expression of the more mature poet.[16] This first period contains the type of poetry which has often caused the critics in general to speak of the influences of Romanticism and especially of Bécquer, in his adolescent poetry. Although the poetic production of Silva was not heterogeneous or equal in artistic value, in the second period his poetry took on a new maturity of style lasting until his death. However, in the analysis of Silva's poetry in this work, the chronological division will not be used. The division will be a primarily thematic one.

Even though Silva's early production may be incidental and undeveloped, most of the poems reflect the Romantic influences which characterize Silva's as well as most of the other Modernists' early compositions. Silva was a Romantic by nature, and this inclination was intensified by his reading. He translated three of the poems of French Romantic writers, and these were among the first poems published by Silva. Yet the Romantics of his own and other Spanish-American countries were not without influence on him. His first poems were simple in vocabulary and showed a direct and often sentimental emotion. However, the critic Luis Alberto Sánchez says that Silva lived on the border of two different modes: Romanticism, and the "decadent," which was the beginning of Modernism.[17]

II *Childhood with Its Joys and Sorrows*

In this first thematic division of poems, childhood is evoked with its innocence, although at times looking to the future and foretelling a loss of purity. In the poem "Infancia" (Infancy) (pp. 31–33), his understanding of the period of idyllic happiness (p. 33) is clear, but he is also obviously looking back on these "breves dichas transitorias" (brief, transitory joys) from a later

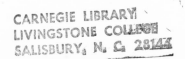

period when the disillusionments of life loom larger. He speaks
of childhood, "Donde es süave el rayo/Del sol que abrasa el
resto de la vida" (Where the rays are gentle/of sun which
parches the rest of life) (p. 33). This "edad feliz" (happy age)
(p. 32) is in Silva's life one of the memories with which he re-
creates a peace he never felt in the remainder of his life. Yet
because it is only a memory, the feeling of melancholy is always
present. For Silva ". . . el recuerdo vago de las cosas/que em-
bellecen el tiempo y la distancia" (. . . the vague remembrance
of events/which time and distance beautify) (p. 31) idealizes
the past. The ambiguous and the vague images allow the reader
to recreate his own childhood. In this way Silva produces a poem
of indistinct outlines. The impressions are given by multiple
suggestions to the physical senses, rather than by a minute description of childhood.

Also in "Los Maderos de San Juan" (The Wood of Saint John)
(pp. 35–36) we observe the same mixture of the joys of childhood
with the premonitions of future pain on the part of the grandmother, who is rocking the child on her knee as she sings the
popular children's rhyme. Depth and power are added to the
poem because the poet is able to restate triumphantly the faith
of innocence, broadened by a full recognition of the counter-
claims of experience. The children's rhyme used as a refrain adds
poignancy to the point of view of the grandmother who has lived
and suffered many years.

Several critics have analyzed this poem on the basis of the
time differential in each of the stanzas. There is the period of
the author who returns in memory to his childhood and remembers the romps with his grandmother, but he also reflects a
projection into the future by the grandmother who fears for the
child's future. The poet returns to the present and meditates
upon the present after the grandmother's death. To the memory
of the grandchild who is now an adult "todo el poema triste de
la remota infancia" (All the sad poem of faraway childhood)
(p. 36) returns.

The protagonist in this poem is not solely a catalyzing agent
for the fluidity of time, but is a key image for the embodiment
of a conflict within opposing realities. The poet is torn between
the idea of the joys of childhood and the painful present of

adulthood, just as was the grandmother prefiguring the child's future.

In "Crepúsculo" (Twilight) (pp. 37–39), fairy tales are being told to a little group of children by a voice which is "leve,/argentada y pura" (high, silvery and pure) (p. 38). The scene is set in the afternoon, before the lamp is lit, when dusk is falling. The poet evokes the storytelling hour and the children's rapt attention, and then reflects on the power of these stories: "Cuentos más durables que las convicciones/De graves filósofos y sabios escuelas" (Stories more durable than the convictions/Of sober philosophers and wise schools) (p. 39). These are the stories ". . . que atesoran del sueño poético/El íntimo encanto, la esencia y el germen" (. . . which treasure in them of the poetic dream/The intimate enchantment, the essence and the germ) (p. 39).

For Silva, childhood was one of the most eloquent and touching poetic themes. He evokes it as one of the ages of life when the continuity of the universe and of history is learned intuitively, before cognitive learning has taken place. Fairy tales are a type of dynamic eternity because they go back to faraway times of man and his history, and are repeated by present and future generations. These stories are a kind of connection since they have existed in all ages, and in this way past and present extend into the future.

"Primera Comunión" (First Holy Communion) (p. 105), although written at the age of ten, is not usually placed with Silva's childhood poems. It is an evocation of the special atmosphere of the first communion, with its childish faith and optimism in future virtue, and of the feeling of happines which comes from an act as holy as any which a human being can carry out. In this poem there are no feelings of the disillusionments which will come later in the life of the poet. His faith is real, and is accentuated by the word-painting of the scene where reality smiles at the children before the altar in their mystic purity. Even the paintings of the saints from their dark canvasses "bajo el polvo de siglos que los cubre/mudos se sonreían" (beneath the dust of centuries which covers them/silently were smiling) (p. 105). Although written at an early age, this poem shows some of the techniques which later are exhibited in various poems, such as the use of paintings in two different ways. First, he used the whole poem as a painting of a scene, and at the same time the paintings on the walls of the church add another dimension to the scene.

Silva treats childhood as a land of fantasy and a realm which has to be destroyed as the child becomes the reasoning adult. It is a fluid and brightly colored epoch where flowers move, animals talk, and reason does not put limits on these fantasies. These times are never forgotten, and adults on hearing these old stories are transported back into the world of fantasy, although they no longer believe it exists. On hearing such stories the adult abandons the rational attitude and enjoys the reprieve from his prison of reasonableness. Child psychologists testify that the imagination suffers at the expense of reason, which serves as a restraint, and listening to such stories causes the hearer to break momentarily the bonds of this restraint.

"Al Pie de la Estatua" (At the Foot of the Statue) (pp. 39–50) fits under several of the thematic categories into which this chapter is divided. However, since it is Silva's longest poem, 331 lines, a summary of its content will be given here, before the analysis of the theme of childhood appearing in parts of it. The summary follows:

The poem is dedicated to Caracas on the day of the national holiday of Venezuela, and was recited by Silva in Bogotá at a reception given by the Minister of Venezuela.[18] The poet describes the statue of Bolívar by Tenerani which is located in the plaza in front of the cathedral in Bogotá. He speaks of the nobility of expression and of the melancholy posture of Bolívar. He describes the garden around the statue and a group of children noisily playing there. Then he judges that the scene inspires only those who feel a strong sense of patriotism. He points out that the poet who looks at the statue and converses with the soul of things is the first to see the majesty of the work of art which will not be destroyed by time. Returning to the past, the poet speaks of the generations of Indians, the Spaniards who came, and laments that many of them left no sign or memory after living out their lives. But he believes that one single generation (that of Bolívar) redeemed Spanish America and gave the poets many heroic acts to write about.

The poets are told many things they can use to make the Father of Liberty even better known. Silva advises the poets that they not evoke the moments of Bolívar's victories, and that they talk not of his best hours but of his defeats, when in spite of the odds he continued to persevere. All the worst should be told, including the "porvenir de luchas y de horrores/Que le aguarda a la América Latina" (future of struggles and of horrors/Which is ahead for Latin America) (p. 46). By telling of the worst hours of Bolívar, his memory will be purified, and his greatness, in spite of his moments of failure, will be increased. The poet discloses that an outstanding heroic poem about Bolívar has already been written by Miguel Antonio Caro. He was much more successful than the present generation of poets which is "como enfermizo descendiente/De alguna fuerte raza" (like sickly descendants/Of some strong race) (p. 48). Silva addresses Bolívar to tell him that his memory will reach the future even without the compositions of the Modernist poet's generation. He states that Bolívar's glory does not need their poetry. In his conclusion, the poet glances around the garden, where the children are playing and shouting at the foot of the statue, and thinks that the monument in its epic glory will be there long after the children are dead.

The theme of childhood is present in the contrast between the innocent children playing around the statue and the bitterness which Bolívar felt in his later days. The playing children are juxtaposed with the serious Father of the Country, the hero of the South American Republics. The children do not understand suffering as yet, and do not feel the poignancy or the loneliness which the epic hero suffered. But whether or not they understand, the monument to his glory will outlast their lives, and will withstand the passage of time long after they are dead.

III   *Education and Its Disillusionments*

Education, especially self-education, is one of Silva's principal disillusionments in life because of its doubt-raising propensities, and because it does not give emotional happiness. In the poet's view education could give intellectual satisfaction, but solely if it were carried out with pedagogical order. But in his case it did not happen, since he was forced to leave school and to obtain his education by reading.

Being a self-taught intellectual, as was Silva, is at one and the same time a detriment and a benefit. Whoever reaches it feels superior to others, and this superiority endows that person with a fuller capacity to suffer. One feels that an intellectual should have gained a universal panacea, but happiness is difficult for such a person to obtain. Also, intellectual life in the days of Silva had already reached a state of enormous complexity. The influence of learning upon increasing spiritual desolation has been known since remote times; Ecclesiastes says: "Who gains education gains sorrow." And in Silva's time, because of man's already elaborate civilization, true laughter was not possible, for man is a sad and melancholy creature. Both men of action and of thought are equally sad, and laughter is possible only for primitive peoples.

The poem "Piscopatía" (Mental Disorder) (pp. 73–77), from "Cenizas" (Ashes), attacks the idea of the capability of man to think and reason as the cause of his lack of satisfaction. Although this poem seems bitter enough to be one of the "Gotas Amargas" (Bitter Potions), Silva listed it under "Cenizas" in the manuscript he prepared. In this narrative poem, a doctor and his daughter are strolling in the park, where a young man dressed in black is walking and thinking. The scene is painted in all the color and light of a spring morning, but the young philosopher does not even see the beauty around him. The daughter asks what illness the youth has. Her father tells her that it is an ailment which rarely attacks women and only occasionally men: "Sufre este mal: . . . pensar . . ., esa es la causa/De su grave y sutil melancolía" (He suffers this illness: . . . thinking . . . , that is the cause/Of his sober and subtle melancholy) (p. 75).

The physician informs his daughter that in past ages the treatment for such diseases has been prophylactic, burning these thinkers at the stake or putting them in prisons. But now the same treatment cannot be used. The doctor tells his daughter that he has cured only two such cases. The only cure for them is to stop thinking and clear the mind of ideas, to throw themselves actively into a life of physical labor or to resign themselves to suffer until death comes. But this youth is a difficult case, and according to the physician will "pasar diez años con los locos" (spend ten years with the insane) (p. 76), and will not be cured until the day "En que duerme a sus anchas/En una angosta sepultura fria" (When he is sleeping restfully/In a narrow, cold sepulcher) (p. 77).

The thinker has been poisoned by his reading, by the criticism of all ideas and all hopes in life. His only two alternatives are these: to deny his education, to stop using it and let it atrophy while he plunges into a job of mindless activity; or to suffer, in or out of the insane asylum, until he reaches death.

In the poem from "Gotas Amargas," "El Mal del Siglo" (Malady of the Century) (pp. 88–89), the patient describes his intellectual ailment to the doctor. He is tired of everything; he feels an incessant "renegar de lo vil de la existencia/ digno de mi maestro Schopenhauer" (abhorrence of the vileness of existence/worthy of my master Schopenhauer) (p. 88). But the doctor has no answer for him except that he should regularize his physical life. His diagnosis is not so far from the correct one: hunger, not hunger of the body, but hunger of the spirit, for peace which cannot be found. Again the advice of the poet is to leave the intellectual life and enter into a regimen which concentrates not upon the mental processes, but the physical, forgetting the ideas the young man might have learned from his reading and study. Self-analysis is not good for these persons since the torture of seeing clearly their own pessimism augments the torture and suffering.

"Lentes Ajenos" (Borrowed Spectacles) (pp. 90–92) shows the same disillusionment with the process of self-education through reading. Juan de Dios tried out several different patterns of love he discovered in the books he read, and with each succeeding one became unhappier. The commentary of the poet is that Juan de Dios always loved through books and probably "nunca supo lo que es amor" (never knew what love is) (p. 92). The conclusion one might reach upon considering this poem is that Silva was being very ironical, since rarely would anyone pattern his love life after books. In a way he is more than ironical, he is bitter, not so much about love itself, but about everything learned from literature which cannot be helpful when applied to the life of man. For Silva there is no inspiration for true love in literature.

IV   *The Impossible Search for Virtue*

In "Don Juan de Covadonga" (pp. 77–80), from "Cenizas," the eponymous hero of the narrative poem goes to visit his elder brother Hernando, prior of a convent, to search for religious consolation. Don Juan has already spent a great deal of his life in dissipations and has only found melancholy as a result. He has decided to abandon the life he has led and enter the religious life, only to learn from the prior that the life there in seclusion is a constant battle against sinful desires for the pleasures of a life similar to the one led by his worldly brother. Upon hearing this, Don Juan does not feel there will be any benefit in telling his brother that he came there to enter into the monastic life. He thinks to himself that he must have been mad to have believed that life might be virtuous within the religious orders. But one can observe that it was his last hope since as he leaves "Por primera vez se humedecieron/Los ojos de don Juan de Covadonga" (For the first time tears came to/The eyes of Don Juan de Covadonga) (p. 80). There is no possibility of contentment for man. There is not even a way to be virtuous, and Don Juan leaves with a mortal sadness, for he knows he is condemned to continue in the same boring excesses of the flesh which do not bring happiness.

"Perdida" (Lost) is one of the poems not usually added to the editions of Silva's poetry.[19] It explains the situation of a young working girl who has lost her virtue. She gives in to her seducer, and is left one day in the street with a child in her arms and her honor lost. She resorts to prostitution to wreak her vengeance upon men. But her vengeance is short-lived for she becomes prematurely old, and ill, and dies in the hospital. The final stanza is an indictment by the poet of the infamous libertine who is responsible for her fall, but without any hope that his conscience might bother him because of what had happened, or that he would ever feel sorry for the child whom he can never call his son. The poem ends with the repetition of the first four lines:

Algo terrible sentirá tu alma	(Rather terrible your soul must feel,
Infame libertino,	Infamous libertine,
Que el taller tornas de la	Who turns the workshop of the poor
pobre obrera	working girl
En lupanar maldito!	Into a cursed brothel!) (p. 142)

This poem is more literal than most of Silva's poems and shows the poet's sorrow concerning the niggardly conscience of some men who are responsible at times for the difficult existence of women who become prostitutes. And yet, nature is surely the cause of these tragedies. The sentimental and physiological force of the erotic has caused the fall of the girl. And whether or not the seducer feels as much pain as the poet hopes, the poem reflects the same search for virtue which is impossible to attain for various reasons beyond the control of human beings.

V Amorous and Erotic Poems and Poems about Friendship

Love has traditionally been one of the ways in which humans can escape from their own consciousness. It is a way of gaining comfort because it is consolation, illusion, and gaiety. Love is forgetting the self, the irradiation of the self into the world. But both literature and life show that there is nothing lasting about love or the happiness it briefly brings. In some of Silva's poems love has lost the pleasant qualities it once had. No longer is there the tenderly loving note of an idyll, but rather an intimate disgust, the sadness of the fatigued flesh, the consciousness of the spirit which feels itself destroyed by the concupiscence of sex, and would like to escape but cannot. Humans feel the melancholy of impossible love, of disillusionment with love, the disenchantment and incomprehension between couples, and various aberrations in the relations of heterosexual love.

One poem found under the title "De Gotas Amargas" (From Bitter Potions), which begins "Cayeron las cadenas..." (The chains fell ...),[20] does not have a great deal of proof that Silva was its author. If he was, he changed his style in this poem. Here he has made a different kind of painting, one with harsh sounds and unpoetic words rarely used by Silva. There is none of the bitterness which is the main characteristic in the poems from "Gotas Amargas." It is simply the encounter in a castle of a new page and a girl who is waiting for him with a light for their love-tryst. Until there is further proof that this is by Silva, it has to be judged as questionable. Stylistically it is very unlike any of Silva's other poems.

"A Ti" (To You) (p. 127) is one of the rare compositions by Silva where love lacks the tinge of sinful lust. The poet looks upon the union of the flesh as a happy moment when two souls are united and when both feel the nearness of the infinite through their loving union. Similarly, "Poesía Viva" (Living Poetry) (pp. 123–25) is also a poem in which there is no sense of desperate pessimism or of disillusionment with love. The scene portrayed is that of a young married couple with a tiny baby, at home in the evening. The husband is a poet and he is contemplating the scene of his young wife dreaming beside the cradle of the child. He reads to her a poem which was inspired by his trust in life that has arisen from "estos días risueños,/de nuestros meses queridos" (these smiling days,/of our loving months) (p. 124). With his loved ones beside him he is not frightened by the night. But when he looks to his wife to discover what her emotions are upon hearing the poem, he discovers that she has gone to sleep. In the final three stanzas (found by this author and others),[21] the poet sadly lets the poem fall and listens to an interior emotion which is stronger than his verbalization of the scene or of the emotions felt.

In two poems the *carpe diem* idea appears and is approached in a slightly different way. One, which has an interrogation sign for a title and which begins "¿Por qué de los cálidos besos..." (Why from the fiery kisses...) (p. 128), reflects the hedonistic idea. First the poet questions why the excesses of the flesh are harmful to those who engage in them, often bringing death. Then he questions whether the ascetics are wise for living in cells adorned only with a cross and four bones. The answer he gives is a call to all humans to enjoy carnal pleasures, to experience all fleshly joys possible since no matter what kind of life one lives, everyone ends up in "las negruras de la tierra" (the blackness of the earth) (p. 128). In "El Alma de la Rosa" (The Soul of the Rose) (pp. 122–23), the flower worn by the girl to the dance tells the story of its brief life span and its death, withering on the shoulder of the girl at the dance. The poet suggests that not only the rose loses its bloom in a short time, but that the beauty of the girl is fleeting as well, and therefore life must be enjoyed to the fullest in the years of youth and grace.

The poem which begins "Oh dulce niña pálida ..." (Oh pale, gentle lass ...) (pp. 121–22) has been given several different titles by editors. The first edition has it listed as "Nocturno IV," but Silva never intended to call it this since he did not give it this title as he did the other three "Nocturnos" in the text or in the table of contents of the facsimile of his manuscript. Other editors have used the first four words as a title, and some have called it "Dime" (Tell Me). Some critics classify it among the "Gotas Amargas." It could well be one of those sarcastic poems, since it is a bitter question addressed to a young and innocent girl who has never been approached with lustful thoughts, and whose lips have only opened to pray. The poet asks the girl if while sleeping she were to feel the kiss of the youth with whom she had danced and enjoyed herself, whether or not she would be overcome by emotion and awaken to respond actively. The poet implies that she is a coquette, in a sense, because of her lack of understanding of the depths of emotion she awakens in her dancing partner, making him desire her and suffer because of his feelings.

"Mariposas" (Butterflies) (p. 61) is an extended metaphor in which the collection of butterflies of the loving girl are likened to the desires visible in her eyes, in that they seem to live anew when they are touched by the sun. But in the description of the butterflies, "fijas para siempre" (mounted permanently) (p. 61), is reflected the desire of the poet to be able to mount in a stable way things other than butterflies. Here is the vision of the poet of a world in constant change. The symbolism of flux, which the poet would like to stop, is concentrated in the process of metamorphoses from ugly cocoons to beautiful butterflies. He would like to mount for all time the lovely things he sees. He implies that he would like permanence in love, as well as in life; that they be fixed for always, unchanging.

"Juntos los Dos" (We Two Together) (p. 51) has sometimes been published with the title "Risa y Llanto" (Laughter and Tears). The second title manifests the antithesis of tears turning into a feeling of enchantment, and of laughter turning into tears.

In this poem about love, the poet considers that from joyous orgies are born "hondos suspiros" (deep sighs) (p. 51). He admits that from the salty waters of the ocean come the white pearls and that, metaphorically speaking, from tears come emotions of great value. Thus from pleasant things come unpleasant ones, and vice versa.

Poem number X of the group called "Notas Perdidas" (Lost Notes), which begins "¿Has visto, cuando amanece..." (Have you seen, when at sunrise . . .),[22] is dedicated to Natalia Tanco A[rmero]. It is a light poem of friendship. In an extended metaphor, the poet compares the frost on the windows, turned into visions by the heat of the sun's rays, to her smile, which turns the mists of sadness into pure white visions.

Another of the "Notas Perdidas," which unlike the others has no number and begins "Es media noche . . ." (It's midnight . . .),[23] is an idyllic love poem. Adriana is dreamily playing the piano and the poet suggests ineffable meditations which cause her to sigh. The poet addresses Adriana and concludes that the room, the moonlight rays, and the silent night will preserve the memories of such pleasant hours and of the "ruido de tus besos" (sound of your kisses) (p. 146).

In the "Nocturno" which begins "A veces cuando en alta noche tranquila..." (At times when in deep and tranquil night...) (p. 52), there is again a girl playing the piano in a romantic love poem. The poet dreams that they both return to the past, to a castle where the two of them watch the sunset. They look at each other and smile, and on returning to reality, the poet thinks with a note of sadness: "¡Cómo tendéis las alas, ensueños vanos,/Cuando sobre las teclas vuelan sus manos!" (How you spread your wings, vain dreams,/When over the keys her hands fly!) (p. 53).

Poem number IV of the "Notas Perdidas," which begins "La noche en que al dulce beso..." (The night in which to the sweet kiss . . .),[24] presents a young couple walking on the night of their first kiss, a beautiful night when the Milky Way is visible. The youth asks the girl if she is tired of walking. She replies that even if it took centuries "Esa distancia infinita/ Feliz, contigo cruzara" (That infinite distance/Happily, I would cross with you!) (p. 147).

Another light, sentimental poem, "Nupcial" (Nuptial) (p. 62), treats the scene of a marriage ceremony. The couple is described in their gaiety which is echoed in the sound of the bells. The dance at the reception with all its sights, sounds, and smells is depicted. But as the couple prepares to depart, a note of sadness and melancholy is given by the sunset and the violin music.

Contrasting with these sentimental poems without eroticism is the "Nocturno" which begins "Poeta, di paso . . ." (Poet, say softly . . .) (pp. 53–54). It exists in two versions in the handwriting of the poet, one entitled "Nocturno," and the other "Ronda" (Night Watch), with some differences in the text but without major changes. It has been given all three titles mentioned above by the different editors, and one editor used "Besos" (Kisses). In the poem there are three scenes. The first one is the loving sexual union of the protagonist and a girl out in the forest. In the second, the following nights in the bedroom are described in all their colorful splendor and sensuality. The final scene is the night when the girl lies dead in her coffin, and the smell of mignonette still permeates, as it did in the previous two scenes. Death has destroyed their love, and the tragic view of life recurs in which everything must come to an end, leaving nothingness and extreme boredom. The idea of *carpe diem* is suggested, since death comes all too soon.

In the following five poems from "Gotas Amargas" Silva reflects upon the sad aspects of sensuality and of human love. In his exhibition of psychic and carnal intimacies, the poet demonstrates a strong kinship with writers of the latest poetry who go much further than did Silva.

"Enfermedades de la Niñez" (Maladies of Childhood) (pp. 93–94) manifests the sadness of sensuality, ironically, even in the title. The poem represents the first encounter of a young man with a "vieja cortesana" (an old prostitute) (p. 94). While he has been dreaming of a delectable and divine ecstasy, the caresses leave him "melancólico y mohino" (melancholy and depressed) (p. 94). The youth finds that "Del amor no sintió la intensa magia . . ." (From love he never felt the intense magic . . .) (p. 94), and was given a venereal infection.

"Madrigal" (p. 93) portrays a beautiful girl and ironically ends with this view of her femininity: "todo esto está, y a gritos, pidiendo un hombre" (All this is shrieking for a man) (p. 93). Woman is considered to be a mindless creature, made for the pleasure of man, who can only be fulfilled in that manner. There is no recognition of the girl as a human being with a brain capable of thinking, but as a sex-object only, and unfortunately this is often the case with exceptionally beautiful girls.

"Egalité" (p. 103) approaches sensuality from another direction, demonstrating that man is a slave to his sexual instinct, very similar to animals in heat, which is a process of nature they cannot counteract. Thus all men are the same, no matter how high or low each man's station may be in life: "es absolutamente igual...los dos son un mismo animal" (he is absolutely equal... both are the same animal) (p. 104).

"Idilio" (Idyll) (p. 103) ironically shows that for the poet love was one of the most transient emotions. The couple who adored each other ended the relationship. Instead of her dying of a broken heart, she died of a miscarriage. Nor was the young man's end romantically tragic. He did not commit suicide, but "Se casó seis meses antes/del matrimonio de ella, y es feliz" (He was married six months before/her marriage, and is happy) (p.103).

"Cápsulas" (Capsules)[25] alludes to the medicines taken by Juan de Dios who, after the ecstasies of love with Aniceta, has a venereal disease. While in love with Luisa he catches tuberculosis and has to take other medicines to be cured. Love brings illness and disenchantment with life for Juan de Dios. But after being cured from those illnesses, the protagonist finds an incurable one when he becomes a philosopher and reads Leopardi and Schopenhauer. The capsules he takes for that more serious disease are "las cápsulas/de plomo de un fusil" (the capsules/ of lead from a gun) (p. 93).

VI   *Meditations on the Essence of Life*

The last stanza of the previously discussed poem, "Cápsulas" (p. 92), answers a question posed by the poet concerning the essence of human existence. Life was without value for Juan de Dios after he became a "filósofo sutil" (subtle philosopher) (p. 93). But the poet does not always find answers for the questions he asks about life, as in the poem "La Respuesta de la Tierra" (The Earth's Answer) (pp. 89–90), also from "Gotas Amargas." Here we see the poet-priest who asks the earth answers concerning the essential nature of life, the reasons for birth and death. But "La Tierra, como siempre, displicente y callada,/al gran poeta lírico no le contestó nada" (The Earth, as always indifferent and silent,/did not reply to the great lyric poet). This poem has been interpreted in three different ways: 1) that it represents Silva;[26] 2) that it is a satire of a poet who is pantheistic and talks to all the stars and the elements;[27] 3) that it was inspired by a poem by François Coppée[28] by the same title.[29] As in the poem by Coppée the egocentric protagonist questions the earth. Coppée's protagonist is a Chinese emperor taking part in an annual ceremonial plowing rite to enable him to receive answers from the Earth. There is the same lack of response in the two poems, although the answer in Coppée is the appearance of a skull in one of the furrows. Silva has written an original poem using some of the ideas which Coppée used.

"Resurrexit"[30] has been included in a few of the subsequent editions probably because of its clear attack on religious beliefs. The title refers to the resurrection of the flesh and spirit. But the poem denies the possibility of such an afterlife, and stresses the idea of *carpe diem*, since there is no other life. Here the poet is more bitterly scornful of some of the beliefs held by Christians. He seems to want to wound the reader by counseling that there be no repentance and that pleasure be searched for in the relations of the flesh. Even the biblical Magdalena is satirized since she is depicted as a go-between for deceased virgins. The only afterlife according to the poet is a kind of pantheistic union with nature or Nirvana.

"Armonías" (Harmonies)[31] is a variation of the poem "Resurecciones" (Resurrections) (pp. 60–61), with two lines exactly the same as the first couplet of the poem, and with one line having only one word changed. However, "Armonías" has three stanzas which follow, different from "Resurecciones." An extended metaphor likens nature to the human soul with its "silencios, luces, músicas y sombras" (silences, lights, music and shadows) (p. 150). In the soul the clouds are illusions which are dissipated by the sun of reality, just as in nature. Everything is born and everything dies in nature and in the soul. And in nature, flowers sprout from the tombs of the deceased, while in the soul, when love has died, dreams of mystic sadness are produced.

In the poem whose title is usually given as a question mark, or "Estrellas" (Stars) (pp. 62–63), first there is a word painting of the universe with the stars in its midst. The poet tries to give an idea of the immense infinity which cannot really be encompassed by the human imagination. But this was not the poet's sole aim, and he asks: "¿Por qué os calláis si estáis vivas/Y por qué alumbráis si estáis muertas?" (Why are you silent if you are alive/And why do you give light if you are dead?) (p. 63). Here the stars represent a problem or a metaphysical question asked by the poet. His interrogation is rather simple in that he uses not philosophical investigation but poetic intuition laced with rational truth. The questions are often dissipated in vague and dreamy meditation and often not expressed except with synthetic appositions, as in the phrase: "Estrellas, luces pensativas" (Stars, pensive lights) (p. 63).

In another poem, "A un Pesimista" (To a Pessimist) (p. 126), Silva ironically expresses an optimistic feeling concerning life. This poem was evidently written in a period of euphoria in which the future does not seem so dark to the poet. At least there are some compensations: "algo tiene de plácido la vida" (life has some tranquility) (p. 126). Even though there are "angustiosas decepciones" (anguished disappointments) (p. 126), life in the future offers the promise of the tenderness of a wife and children.

In "Psicoterapéutica" (Psychotherapy) (p. 94), one of the "Gotas Amargas," the poet counsels bitterly that if one wishes to live a long life in good health to "ten desde niño desengaños,/ practica el bien, espera el mal" (begin having disappointments in childhood,/do good and expect evil) (p. 94). He suggests with tongue in cheek that one should follow the norm of doing the natural thing. In an ironic twist, the poet urges that one avoid the teaching of the philosophers, and in a final shocking metaphor advises that love be avoided: "... aplícate buenos cauterios/ en el chancro sentimental" ("... apply good cauterizing agents/ to the sentimental chancre) (p. 94).

"Futura" (Future) is one of Silva's "Gotas Amargas" and is often given without the final three stanzas. However, the poem seems more complete in meaning if the last stanzas are added. The subject of the poem is the projected time in the twenty-fourth century when a statue of Sancho Panza is erected in a Frankfurt plaza and is called founder and apostle of the religion of the future. The monument is unveiled of the image of the god proclaimed by man as the only one for four centuries. In the last three stanzas the poet presents the nihilism and iconoclasm of an unbelieving people who destroy with dynamite the statue and the orator. This poem presents the disillusionment of Silva with the existing material values in life and projects them, multiplied, into the future.

Another of the pessimistic "Gotas Amargas," "Zoospermos" (Sperm) (pp. 97–100), displays Silva's intellectual disillusionment with scientific pursuits. A scientist who has dedicated his life to the study of sperm dies poor and forgotten in the insane asylum. He has ruined his nerves and has nearly gone blind while studying spermatozoa under the microscope. He pessimistically imagines what life would be like for some of the sperm. Silva's discontent with life is reflected in the words of the investigator to the sperm, ironically saying that fortunately they will not live to fill the earth with joys or horrors, that it is a good thing that "dentro de diez minutos/todos estaréis muertos" (within ten minutes/you will all be dead) (p. 99).

"Voz de Marcha" (Marching Song) (pp. 109–11) is a more optimistic meditation on life. The poem has a Becquerian tone and a similarity to Bécquer's themes. The protagonist is a young man already tired of human existence and without hope for the future. As he sits by the side of the road he hears a voice which gives him the advice that he follow his route as though he were a pilgrim, onward, always onward. He is told that perhaps in this way the future, which seems so dark now, will be brighter, that from difficult times come advantages for the human being. He hears that stimulating marching song in his ears: "pensad que sólo sois un peregrino . . . /Y ¡Seguid adelante!" (think that you are only a pilgrim . . . /And Follow onward!) (p. 111). It stimulates the young man to arise and begin anew his travels through life with some consolation and optimism that things might turn out well for him.

"Al Pie de la Estatua" (At the Foot of the Statue) (pp. 39–50), written in 1895, does not evoke the triumphs of the hero but rather his failures and defeats, his hours of bitterness, his humanness. It is not truly an epic poem, then, or even a heroic poem. The poet himself enters the poem and his situation in the present is compared with the life of the heroic yet human Bolívar. This was a new kind of poetry about heroes for the South American continent, a kind which did not see ahead the brilliant future often expected as the next stage after freedom from Spanish colonialism. Destiny is not quite so favorable, but more realistic. For the social and political epoch, probably a truly heroic poem in traditional style would have been preferable as a method of teaching patriotism and heroism. However, Guillermo Valencia speaks of the poems dedicated to Bolívar and says Silva's would be the best if Miguel Antonio Caro had not written a better one.[32]

The disillusionment of Silva is clear when he states that his generation is incapable of writing epic poetry or even heroic poetry. Some critics have said that this poem was not really apropos for the social and political conditions of his time, but the poet was apolitical and rarely concerned himself with such things. He felt his ineptitude for doing anything positive for his country. Silva synthesizes his view of the destruction of heroic ideals. For the poet these ideals only existed during the generation of Bolívar and the other patriots who fought for freedom. He implies that existence is useless, and that in present and future generations life will be ruled by oppressive nothingness. There is the idea of human impotence combined with the concept of "vanity, all is vanity." These sentiments create desperation in humans, except for the poet who delights in his own pain and suffering, for in that way only, he knows he is alive.

In "Filosofías" (Philosophies) (pp. 100–102), from "Gotas Amargas," love, pleasure, and riches all end in failure and disillusionment. Art is repaid by indifference and forgetfulness. Religion offers only doubtful hopes. Reason destroys all beliefs and even faith in oneself. All activity, even that of doing nothing, as the yogi in his meditations, is only a source of anguish. This poem is a strongly worded negation of everything in life with a bitter and absolute hopelessness. The poet sarcastically challenges all hope, beliefs, and ideas of human beings. He was an idealist, a searcher for the impossible who doubted everything and had come to believe life was useless. His suicide proves that these expressions of futility were not a pose.

In all these poems we have seen that in his pessimistic outlook on life Silva does not enjoy that pessimism. He rather suffers from the metaphysical problem without resolving it. It causes him pain and chains him to it. But Silva cannot accept it; he can only suffer with an impotent desire to rebel. His drama is that of not being able to accept his pessimism. He has absorbed the main characteristics of contemporary thought, but has transformed them into an original position.

"Gotas Amargas" reflect one mode of his feelings, the low ebb of his struggle against pessimism. They seem more sophisticated than other poems, yet there is an echo of personal suffering, scornful rather than bitter. The most profound note of those bitter poems is his refusal to accept the reality of the destruction of his illusions. But behind most irony and satire is a frustrated idealism, the more frustrated, the more satirical.

VII *Time, the Destroyer of the Memory of Loved Ones*

"Luz de Luna" (Moonlight) (pp. 69–71) seems to be a part of a more lovingly treated section of verses separated from "Dia de Difuntos" (Day of the Dead) (pp. 80–84). There is an ambience of destruction of chronological time within one of the favorite themes of Silva: the fleetingness of memory. It reflects the negative feelings of the poet toward the passage of time, which destroys cherished memories. Silva felt that one should not capitulate to time by allowing the destruction of memory, as has the young widow in the poem. The protagonist of the poem is thinking of the party the previous night to which he accompanied the bereaved girl, and there is a suspension of time as he remembers the past, with the couple's newlywed happiness, then the illness and death of her husband only one year ago. Returning in memory to the night of the party, he marvels at the forgetfulness of the young woman, her enjoyment of the party and obliviousness to her past sorrow when her husband died. There is a progressive time sequence from the remote past to the near past to the present and vice versa.

Silva is destructively ironical in "Día de Difuntos" (pp. 80–84). Fiercely and brutally, the poet dissects the human heart with its ingratitude and insatiable desire for pleasure. The poet reflects on the inevitable extinction of memory, especially of the sorrow felt on the death of loved ones. Yet forgetfulness grows within the heart and soul just as the weeds and grass grow in the cemetery. And death is not solely physical but is accompanied by the tragic oblivion. The bells which sound the death knell and the bell which sounds the time of day are contrasted. In an apostrophe to the bells of death the poet says that they should not give in to time, that they should not allow time to conquer memory. But in desperation the poet asks: "Contra lo impossible ¿qué puede el deseo?" (Against the impossible, what can desire do?) (p. 81). Silva documents a universal impermanence with a sweeping vision of change and disillusionment. Time is an inevitable force carrying all things to their death.

The anguish expressed is emphasized by the varying line lengths, giving an irregular rhythm similar to the faltering voice of someone expressing sorrow or loss. Often compared with the famous "Nocturno" are the techniques used in this poem: repetition, onomotopoeia, alliteration, and internal rhymes. These same techniques are also used by Edgar Allan Poe, and for that reason the two poems by Silva have been compared with "The Bells" by Poe. Although Silva uses some of these literary practices, there the likeness ends. Poe writes poems which are disturbingly regular in beat, while Silva uses a great deal of variation, giving a newness to each line. Several students of Silva, such as Arturo Torres Rioseco,[33] continue to dwell on the influences from Poe which they believe they have found in Silva. However, Poe is a more intellectual poet. Both use the same techniques to evoke a certain mood, but Silva's best poems reflect more deeply felt and intimate feelings than Poe's.

In "Triste" (Sadness) (pp. 72–73), and in the final stanza of "Muertos" (Deaths) (pp. 71–72), Silva reiterates the theme of time as a destroyer of memory of those who are either absent or dead. In the first poem, the intensity of tenderness felt toward loved ones causes memory to return now and then, giving renewed anguish and pain. But these remembrances are fleeting, since the human being finds consolation by thinking of ideas which counteract the mourning thoughts. The final stanza of the second poem is more pessimistic, demonstrating that the effects of time are devastating on tender memories since they can never return from those long-past days. And in the vacuum left in their wake is a profound fatigue similar to that which causes the wounded to give up and die, a tiredness which is vague and sad, like the cloudy memory of that which once was and now no longer exists.

Very closely connected with the theme of time, the destroyer of memories of loved ones, is that of death and the brevity of life. In "Muertos" the first two stanzas speak of three kinds of deaths. One is the death of the trees and vegetation when the cold weather arrives, and the sad foliage says goodbye to the dead summer. In the second stanza, two kinds of death are considered: that of love, symbolized by old love letters, even though the passion which inspired them is long past; and dead, dried-out bunches of flowers. All of these types of death have the sad color and odor of things which once existed in the faraway past.

"En la Muerte de mi Amigo Luis A. Vergara R." (On the Death of my Friend Luis A. Vergara R.)[34] is a poem of elegy dedicated to a friend. Rather conventional, this occasional poem uses a more prosaic vocabulary than Silva normally utilizes to express his ideas in verse. First he dwells on the grave and then on the youth and innocence of the deceased, also a poet, who was virtuous, good, and kind. He left loved ones, a girl he cared for, and his family and friends. Here Silva follows through with his poetic idea that there is a life after death, that: "Cuando el cuerpo perece nace el alma" (When the body perishes the soul is born) (p. 137), an idea that Silva did not accept in later years.

"Resurrecciones," similar in the first stanza to "Armonías" but with a more pessimistic message, reflects on the theme of death enchained with life, one following the other. The final stanza has a similar antithesis to "Armonías," but with much less indication of a childhood faith in a life after death. From the decomposed bodies of corpses, foliage grows, and new religions are formed from the broken altar stones, new beliefs from the broken shreds of religions. But the new things arising from the dead bodies and beliefs do not form a joyous or optimistic image. This is a suggestive poem rendering the immaterial with material images similar to the Symbolists. For Silva life and death are not different or mutually exclusive; on the contrary, they are two points in a continuum of existence in which everything is to be found: men, their feelings, their ideas, their aspirations, their creations which move toward nothingness, toward death. The poet sees this continuum of life and death like a chain whose links are the successive moments of life. He considers his own soul as a process of "pasos inestables" (unstable steps) (p. 60) in the eternal essence of change which rules the universe as well as man.

Silva's longest poem (331 lines) and the last one he wrote, "Al Pie de la Estatua" (At the Foot of the Statue) (pp. 39–50), has some lines in which he considers death. First there is the idea that the statue of Bolívar is the conqueror of death, but in a figurative way in which his glory makes him immortal. Yet Silva remembers the numerous generations of Indians and Spaniards who died and were forgotten completely, without having left a trace, until the generation which gained freedom from Spain earned glory and renown, and for some of them, like Bolívar, immortality. The poet also makes the contrast between the children playing around the statue, who will be dead, and the statue which will continue to stand.

The fame of Silva as a poet continues to be founded firmly on the nocturne "Una Noche" (One Night) (pp. 54–56). The poem is his most original contribution in form and content. Concerning the form, Silva said to Baldomero Sanín Cano that the idea for using the meter with a four-syllable nucleus came from the Spanish writer of verse-fables, Iriarte.[35] The innovation, however, was not wholly the use of the four-syllable nucleus, but was the conscious manner in which he used it. He varies the rhythm, and does not follow a rigid regularity in the four-syllable "foot." He also combines the nucleus into verses of great variation in length, from four syllables to twenty-four. In poetry in Spanish the meter is not measured by feet, but by

syllable count, and regular accentual patterns are rarely main-
tained beyond a few lines.

In "Una Noche," where the poet does not state his pessimistic
feelings concerning death, the desolation shows in other ways.
Often Silva's negation and bitterness lack a moving quality
because there is a certain ostentation which is pleased with
itself. Not in the least sentimental, this poem has expressed the
exacerbated sentiment in elegant, composed forms. There is a
painful sincerity which tries to show the poet's reality of sorrow
and loss. It delves into a personal reality felt by everyone who
has lost someone truly loved. All is united with an absolute
syntactical simplicity, without rhetorical ornamentation. It is a
synthesis which allows the reader to participate in the poetic
creation. The poet creates the symbol of a feeling, not by
recalling objects which would elicit the feeling itself, but by
weaving a pattern of words charged with meaning and colored
by literary associations akin to the dynamic pattern of the feeling.

Using these suggestive methods, the poet indicates his con-
victions concerning the inevitable separation of human beings,
and the isolation he felt after the death of Elvira. She was one
of the few persons who could mitigate in a small way that alone-
ness, and penetrate the solitary interior world of her brother.
Silva returns in memory to the time of her death: "Llena de las
infinitas amarguras y agonías de tu muerte,/Separado de ti
misma, por las sombros, por el timpo y la distancia" (Full of
the infinite bitterness and agony of your death,/Separated from
you by the nightshades, by time and distance) (p. 55). The
poet contemplates the inevitable solitude and isolation of the
human being, who is even more alone when those who understood him are taken by death, after a brief time on earth. Death
was the end of their communion, and the poet remembers with
deep grief that it exists no more, and his pain is all the more
poignant since he does not believe in life after death.

Death of loved ones was the cause of most of Silva's pessimism
due to his agnosticism and his loss of faith in a life after death.
Therefore the theme arose in Silva from an individual preoccupation. Nevertheless, it reflects the prolonged Romantic
tradition in which death was an important theme. But this famous poem is one in which Silva writes vague and suggestive

poetry, similar to Verlaine, which evokes the emotions and their effects by his combinations of simple but profoundly moving words, and words whose everyday connotations are changed to more suggestive meanings. However, in a way this poem is also similar to Mallarmé in his suggestiveness of the pure idea of death and separation which isolate the human being through the brevity of life and the inevitability of death. The poem is a meditation on a subject which makes the poet suffer, and the reader also, as he reads or recites the poem. Silva uses all the techniques possible to make the narration more intense in every way. Perhaps he is somewhat masochistic in his desire to remember his suffering; or, on the contrary, by creating from his deep grief this moving elegy, he was able to mitigate and soothe in some measure his agony.

In "La Ventana" (The Window) (pp. 117–20), after quoting from Victor Hugo about the splendors of past times, the poet describes a colonial balcony in an old narrow street and imagines the persons who in the past might have been waiting there at the window. But he knows that not even the shadows remain of those people who disappeared long ago, and the noise of children playing surrounds the window. The window does not guard the memories, and only the poet can recreate them, since he alone hears their secret voices, revealing the story of past generations connected with the window. Yet, as he looks at the children playing, the poet meditates on the brevity of life and on the idea that everything will pass, but that the old window may be there longer than the whole lives of the children playing beneath it. They may pass through their childhood, youth, maturity, and old age, and finally sleep in their graves while the window continues in the same place. The poet unites a kind of archeological description of the dust of an accumulation of years with a childish scene, fresh and noisy. By contrast, he obtains the same ponderative sadness concerning the brevity of life, life which is anxious to devour itself. But the colonial window remains unchangeable as if neither the flight of time nor the steps of death affected it. There is also an apparent effort to make time stand still, an evocation of past, present, and future, creating temporal disorientation.

"Suspiro" (Sigh)[36] is dedicated to a friend whom the poet

asks to remember him, but states that if she does she should not search for him here on earth, but in the sepulcher, "Donde se encuentra paz y descanso" (Where peace and rest is found) (p. 133). In "La Ultima Despedida" (The Last Farewell),[37] the poet is more optimistic about there being something besides peace and rest upon dying. First Death is personified, and speaks, saying that although consisting of light, men fear her. The Bodies speak next, saying that they are going to Mother Earth, to the fecund life. Memories disclose that they will live on in the souls of those who were around them in life, and finally the Souls say they will wander in a region of light and purity after the vague shadows and clouds of life (pp. 143–44).

"El Recluta" (The Draftee) (pp. 112–14) ponders the mystery of a seemingly useless life and death. The soldier earns the respect of no one and dies calling out the name of his mother. The poem seems sentimental. It is the swan song of goodbye to a world where not love but evil reigns.

Silva's poem "Lázaro" (p. 69) has been said to have two different sources. It has been considered to be based on the biblical Lazarus, but beginning after his resurrection in John, 11:1–44.[38] Another critic says that the poem is an imitation of a poem by León Dierx.[39] On comparing the two stanzas of Silva with the thirteen of the poem by Dierx[40] one notes that unlike Silva's poem in which there is no explanation of why Lazarus is disullusioned with life four months later and envies the dead people in the cemetery, Dierx makes it clear that it was because of the people's fear of a man raised from the dead. He became an outsider, and therefore Lazarus wished he had never been resuscitated. Silva's poem is therefore more vague and mysterious.

"Estrellas fijas" (Immovable Stars) (pp. 111–12) is a meditation on the consciousness of death that a person who is deceased may or may not have. Silva questions whether his eyes will continue to contain the memories of the light in the eyes of a person he loved. Whether there in the grave his eyes "verán en lo ignorado de la muerte/tus ojos ... destacándose en las sombras" (will see in the unknown which is death/your eyes ... shimmering in the shadows?) (p. 112). This poem demonstrates the feelings often held about the body after death, that the all-too-real body cannot revert to nothingness. But at the same time, the poet and his readers know that it does, and the eyes of the lovers, remaining fixed, are a symbol of constancy, a constancy for which Silva always searched and was never able to find. He seems also to explore the possibility that after death the human consciousness, with its memories of the past, might continue to exist in some manner in the body in decomposition, that consciousness, although diffuse, might not be totally destroyed, a pantheistic idea.

The poem which begins "Bajad a la pobre niña . . ." (Lower the poor girl . . .),[41] which is given the title "Notas Perdidas" (Lost Notes) (pp. 116–17) in all the editions but is actually poem number IV of the section by that name, treats the death of a beautiful young girl in a different way. When she is lowered into her last resting place the poet asks that another grave be dug near hers so that his memories of her affection and of the most tender moments between them may be buried there beside her. Death brings with it forgetfulness and therefore his affections might as well be interred beside her.

"Crisálidas" (Cocoons) (pp. 34–35) was published in 1886 but was considered to have been written before Silva's European trip on the occasion of the death of his sister Inés, then only a child. It is a meditation of death in which appears the popular conception of the soul as a substance comparable to the substance of the body, a substance which lives after the death of the flesh. There is a comparison of the cocoon, with the butterfly who leaves the cocoon, to the child who dies and whose soul leaves the prison of the flesh. The poet ends with the metaphysical question: "Al dejar la prisión que las encierra/¿Qué encontrarán las almas?" (Upon leaving the prison which encloses them/What will the souls find?) (p. 35).

"La Calavera" (The Skull) (pp. 114–15) is a meditation on a skull on the ruined wall of a convent garden. The poet surmises that it might have been the cranium of some exemplary father. But all around the skull he notes the sounds and aromas of life, and the shadows lend the appearance of life to it. But the soul, the elevated spirit, is no longer there and it is now an empty mansion, and the shadows search for that spirit without hope of finding it. Here Silva makes visible his feeling that death was the inevitable end for all those who live, even those who have an exemplary life. This life was the only one he was sure existed, and the symbol of the skull is a message to enjoy the flesh since no one knows what death is.

"Sonetos Negros" (Black Sonnets) (pp. 128–29) consists of one sonnet and two quartets of a second one. Perhaps these were some of those poems which remained after the rest were lost in the sinking of the ship *L'Amerique*. Both are pessimistic with the first one filled with doubts of there being a God there in the heavens. Faith does not help much when it only gives hope for a future life and not for this one, and the poet asks how man continues "el crüel peregrinaje" (the cruel pilgrimage) (p. 129) to find in the uncertain future only forgetfulness of the painful voyage. In the two quartets of the second sonnet, the poet observes that human reason coldly destroys the illusions formerly cherished, and the advice is given to forget those fantasies and search for enjoyment in life.

"La Respuesta de la Tierra" (The Earth's Answer) (pp. 89–90), discussed previously in connection with meditation of life and its essence, also shows a preoccupation with death. The poet asks "¿Qué somos? ¿A do vamos? ¿Por qué hasta aqui vinimos?" (What are we? Where are we going? Why did we come here?) (p. 89). These are metaphysical questions and the one about death has no answer either, except that it is certain that all humans die, and Silva could find no suitable answer as to where he was going when he died.

Silva views death as an irrational end for human beings who passed a life without meaning. Yet at times he considers death to be an end which provides rest and peace finally. At other times he considers that it is solely an irrevocable termination and that for that reason all should live for the day, hedonistically enjoying everything possible every moment. Death is similar to nature in that the processes are the same. All that exists is moving toward nothingness, toward death. Life is brief, and its successive moments are like a chain of events in life. Yet death comes to all things, and usually Silva shows his idea that it is a definitive end, with some indications of a slight belief in the pantheistic union of the flesh and spirit with nature.

VIII   *Old and New Things in Word Paintings*

There is a small group of poems in which Silva uses poems
to paint likenesses of scenes, sometimes with little profundity
behind the representations, and other times combined with
themes of more depth. In these poems which are portraits of
things, Silva expressed material images related directly to his
thought; yet even here, his choice of vocabulary made these
paintings into a collection of beautifully rhythmical sounds, and
thus they are doubly suggestive. He shows an affection for old
things. Like many of the Modernist authors he feels disgust for
the immediate and the known, and a preference for the distant
and unknown.

"Taller Moderno" (Modern Studio) (pp. 64–65) describes
the objects in the studio of an artist in all their color, odor, and
sight impressions, and in the final stanza states that these things
seem to cry out for a poet "Que improvise del cuarto la pin-
tura/Las manchas de color de la paleta") (To improvise a
painting of the room/With the shadings of the colors of the
palette) (p. 65). Some of the still-life poems, like this one,
seem to be purely descriptive and have no sentiments in particular, but sometimes the feeling is veiled, as in the line in the
first stanza, "De un olor de vejeces peregrino" (with a smell of
pilgrim antiquities) (p. 64), which gives a historical dimension.
Not solely a description, but a recreation or evocation of a
moment, not just floating free, but anchored in time. Choice of
images allows additions of emotion and depth by the manner of
choosing words. Often a line seems commonplace at first glance,
but after penetrating, there is an augmentation of sentiment
given to those images by choice of musical words and unusual
placement.

"Vejeces" (Old Things) (pp. 59–60) displays the poet's view
that things of antiquity contain secrets of past times, of lives no
one remembers. Silva endows the objects with lyricism, an ex-
pressionistic technique. The poet introduces himself affectively
into old objects and discloses sentiments which are actually
those of the past by considering the memories connected with
each of these things, memories of the people who lived their
lives surrounded by them. The dreamer finds in the contempla-

tion of these old things a world of confidences which is a beloved world of escape. The objects take the poet back to better, more distant epochs. For that reason, to the poet-dreamer all kinds of old things "son dulces, gratísimas y caras" (are sweet, extremely agreeable and dear) (p. 60).

In "Sus Dos Mesas" (Their Two Tables) (pp. 120–21), the poet catalogs the articles to be found on the table of a single girl, and then of a married one, suggesting a great deal about the life of singleness as opposed to the married state. By the beauty of the articles on her table, one can assume that for Silva the ideal period for woman is in the single state, while the married woman has mostly things which are connected with the physical care of babies, reflecting a basic change in her preoccupations from that of a single girl. The contrast in the two states in a prosaic language gives humor and allows reality to enter into the daily acts of an everyday world which require certain objects in order to live. The poem reflects the absurdity of life in its irony about things and their effect upon the human being.

"Serenata" (Serenade) (pp. 63–64) is similar to a Romantic poem of reminiscence. The melodical refrain which is the first line of each of the three stanzas, "La calle está desierta; la noche fría; . . ." (The street is deserted, the night cold; . . .), uses representational images. Yet they almost lose that value as they are transformed into musical phrases connected with the state of feeling in the poem. The scene is painted in word pictures accompanied by musical themes. The guitar player brings the music into the scene and the music and song of the serenade cause the girl to open the blind. The victory of love is accentuated by the poet in his description of the moonlight, the deserted night, and the music.

IX Dreams

In the poem to which Silva gave a title in English, "Midnight Dreams" (p. 67), there is also a catalogue of things observed by the poet, not in the world around him, but in his dreams. He sees dreams of other epochs, of hopes and glories, and of happiness which has never been his. These dreams file through his room and fill up the corners. A forgotten odor enters to remind him of a moment in the past. He is surrounded by the faces of persons long forgotten and voices he does not remember. After depicting his dream world the poet says: "Los sueños se acercaron, y me vieron dormido,/Se fueron alejando, sin hacerme ruido" (The dreams approached and saw me sleeping,/And began leaving without making noise) (p. 67). Dreams, like the hopes of the young man, vanish without a sign of their appearance except for a vague melancholy. There is an added suggestivity given by their momentary appearance and by the lack of concrete reality of these manifestations of life in dreams.

X Nature

In "Paisaje Tropical" (Tropical Landscape) (p. 68), Silva describes a scene in nature using words to outline and give form to a landscape. The view of the tropical area is more natural than exotic with the canoe being propelled surely and rapidly down the river in the monotonous calm of a voyage, as dusk falls. There is a reflection in the water of another vaulted sky, "rosado y verdeoscuro/En los espejos húmedos del agua" (rosy and dark green/In the humid mirrors of the water) (p. 68). Here there is no statement or suggestion; however, in "Muertos" (Deaths) (pp. 71–72), word pictures are used to set the scene for the appearance in the last stanza of the theme previously discussed: the loss of affection and tenderness, through death. The scenes are: first, the moribund forest when leaves are falling and vegetation is dying. The second describes old, stained letters and dried-out flowers preserved as remembrances. In the second poem Silva has remade the reflective-topographical poem of a scene of nature, transforming the landscape by his shaping imagination.

The poem "Idilio" (Idyll) (pp. 139–40) which begins "Sencilla y grata . . ." (Simple and pleasing . . .),[42] is a straightforward meditation on, and word painting of, the blessed life in the country, but Silva uses all five of the senses in his imagery. When an honorable death terminates a life of labor there in the midst of nature, the poet points out that dignity and simplicity exist in such a life and death.

"Paseo" (Outing)[43] reflects the surroundings of Silva, with a scene probably on the Sabana of Bogotá, where picnics and outings are held. He describes the happy groups gathered here and there and adds the dimension of sound with the typical melancholy music of the *bambuco*. The description of the music is used as a refrain in two of the stanzas, and gives an additional note of sadness to the outing in the country, for the notes sound out and are "¡Alegres para el que ríe/Y tristes para el que llora!..." (Happy for those who laugh/And sad for those who cry!...). The poet is presenting an idea commonly accepted, that most of one's melancholy and sadness depends on subjective rather than outside influences.

"Nidos" (Birds' Nests)[44] is a poem whose authorship has not been proved definitely, but it has a kinship with Silva's poems about nature in which he paints descriptive scenes of landscapes with words. The virgin jungle is described using words and images of light and color, and in that scene appears a bird's nest in an old tree. The life of the birds is exhibited during the day and during the night, idealizing the affectionate care given to the eggs, and the happiness reflected in the songs of the birds caring for the eggs.

Another poem entitled "Crepúsculo" (Twilight)[45] (by the same title as the better-known poem by Silva), is one written in the period before he went to Europe. It is a description of a landscape with a church in the background. The time is at dusk, with the shadows adding a melancholy aspect and giving the scene a strangeness which causes the thoughts to wander in the quiet of the calm hour. This poem was a part of the notebook of adolescent poems mentioned previously.

XI *Themes Related to Poetic Theory*

Like many other poets, Silva has a good number of poems in which he expresses his ideas and theories concerning the function and method of the poetic art. Silva's theories are expressed in an original form, but are neither new nor shocking. They disclose not only Silva's personal theories, but also the most common theories of the epoch in which he wrote poems.

In "Al Oído del Lector" (For the Ear of the Reader) (p. 31), the poet describes what might be called his theory of composition. Poetry is not inspired by active passion but by the sentiment of a vague tenderness such as that inspired by "los niños enfermizos,/los tiempos idos y las noches pálidas" (sickly children,/past times and pale nights) (p. 31). He believes that the spirit can be inspired to write poems only upon being moved to remember previous emotions in times of tranquility. He states that on the contrary: "Cuando el amor lo agita poderoso/Tiembla, medita, se recoge y calla" (When love agitates it [the spirit] powerfully/It trembles, meditates, withdraws and is silent) (p. 31). This theory seems similar to the Becquerian concepts on the value of poetic evocation and on the necessity to remember in tranquility the passion of the moment to attain value in the poem. But when the poet experiences those moments of passion, his feelings are dissolved in tears of joy or sorrow, not conducive to producing poems.

The poem entitled "Futuro" (Future) (pp. 148–49), and dedicated to Rafael Pombo, was written to accompany a group of compositions by friends of Pombo in 1886 to defend him from the attacks of some of his critics.[46] It indicates clearly Silva's belief in the freedom of the individual poet to change from one type of inspiration to another. He asserts that Pombo had every right to change from the inspiration of the past in which he wrote about "El secreto más íntimo del alma" (The most intimate secret of the soul) (p. 149) to a new kind of search for "audacias de la forma" (audacity of form) (p. 149). Silva recognizes that before, Pombo's inspiration was more nationalistic, and that now, in his new manner, he is being laughed about. Silva tells him that he has the freedom to change in his older years and march into the future with the style which suits him best. He assures him that no matter how he writes his poems ". . . tu memoria vivirá con ellas" (. . . your memory will live with them [your verses]) (p. 149).

The four-line poem which begins "Cuando hagas una estrofa, . . ." (When you write a stanza, . . .)[47] stresses in the first two lines that the poem should be unusual enough to serve as an example for the future. In the second two verses, his metaphor is Parnassian in stating that the poem should have ". . . perfiles de mármol de carrara/y solideces de frontón de templo"

(... outlines of Carrara marble/and the solidity of the front of a temple) (p. 150). The underlying idea is that if the poem is to be sculptured and shaped well, it will last and will give the poet immortality.

"Convenio" (Agreement)[48] reiterates the idea expressed in the prose piece by Silva previously discussed, "La Protesta de la Musa" (The Protest of the Muse). The Muse is displeased when the poet writes about sadness and bitterness. The agreement she wishes to make with the poet is to exchange inspiration for butterflies. She urges the poet not to talk of horrors or doubts or of "... tristezas sin causa y de cansancios/Y de odio a la existencea" (... sorrows without cause and fatigues/And hatred of existence) (p. 138). Here the preference of the Muse is clearly for a more optimistic type of poetry.

The untitled poem which begins "Encontrarás poesía..." (You will find poetry . . .)[49] follows the spirit of the previously discussed poem, that inspiration should be more optimistic. The sources of poems should be found in Christian temples, in forests, in memories of love, in the innocence "De las niñas de quince años/En los blancos aposentos, . . ." (Of fifteen-year-old girls/In their white bedrooms, . . .) (p. 144) in the starry nights, but "¡Jamás ... en los malos versos!" (Never ... in harmful poems!) (p. 144).

There are two stanzas which consider poetic theory which may or may not have come from one poem. One begins "¿Para qué quieres versos . . ." (Why do you want verses . . .),[50] and gives an opinion about art contrary to that given at times in the work of Silva. In this instance he says to an unidentified woman that there is no need for poems when within yourself you will find many poems. A good story is better than an elegy and "... mejor que los cantos de vagos temas/Una boca rosada que se sonría" (... better than the poems of vague themes/A rosy mouth which is smiling) (p. 145). Here we again see the idea of *carpe diem*, which at times Silva advocates more than he does expending great effort on art. The second poem (or stanza) begins "Mas quieres versos..." (But you wish verses . . .)[51] and reiterates the idea expressed above that the reader is poetic, but here with the thought that he is going to write verses. Then, when they are read by the person to whom the

poem is dedicated, "tendrán la lumbre diáfana de tus ideas"
(they will have the diaphanous light of your ideas) (p. 145).
This supports Silva's idea expressed by the mouth of José Fernández, protagonist of *De Sobremesa* (After-Dinner Chat), that
half of the effect of the work of art depends on the hearer or
reader.

"Al Pie de la Estatua" (pp. 39–50) is a composition filled with
admonitions for the poet from the author himself, about art and
the type of poems he should write. He enumerates the incidents
he should relate about the life of Bolívar. For example, he
recommends that the poet "... haz el poema sabio/Lleno de
misteriosas armonías" (... make the poem wise/Full of mysterious harmony) (p. 47). In this poem, because of the use
of apostrophe, the poet talks to his double, objectifying his
poetic ideas, and thereby avoiding having to recur to "I" as
subject. Silva uses this mode to communicate his ideas that the
poet is the person who can converse with the soul of things,
and that for the poet only, they have a secret voice. This interior
voice tells the poet to write about death, which comes to all
things, with one exception, the fame of the hero as represented
by the statue. He urges that the inner poet write of Bolívar's
days of anguish and difficulties, which will add to his glory
more than telling of his heroism. But the inner voice says to
the poet that there are no more epic poets, that he is not one,
and that his "... enclenque/Generación menguada" (... weak/
Decimated generation) (p. 48) is not the one to write epic
poetry. He remarks to Bolívar that he does not need poems
written about him in order to gain immortality, that he already
has it because of his history and his monument. He compares
the poems written about Bolívar to the weak cries of the children playing around the statue, who will be dead and forgotten
while the "epopeya de bronce de la estatua" (epic of bronze of
the statue) (p. 50) still immortalizes the glory of the hero.

In "La Voz de las Cosas" (The Voice of Things) (p. 57), the
poet gives a summary of his efforts to enclose in his poem the
essence of things. He does not want to imitate the objects in
their reality, but to create a new reality by understanding the
intimate voice of things only understood by the poets. He desires
to reflect that intimate reality in his poems through a Symbolist

technique of development of multiple associations of words. He wishes to enclose "Frágiles cosas que sonreís" (Fragile things which smile) (p. 57), and here Silva reflects a rejection of direct statement for indirection, for connotative rather than rational meaning. The solemn ritual is gone, and the poet makes an accomplice of the reader. Yet the poet is still the Romantic oracle, the intermediary of supernatural forces, although now conscious of his role. Yet he expresses the difficulty of the practice of the poetic art. The poet is not the creator of words, he has to live their servitude and search for those adequate to the subject he wishes to express.

"Las Arpas" (The Harps)[52] compares the soul of the poet with the Aeolian harp which is silent when the wind does not blow through its strings, just as the poet is silent until sentiment vibrates within him and he "produce sus cantos y sus versos" (produces his songs and his verses) (p. 134). But that production just begins when sentiment vibrates and creates within him the necessary inspiration. Then the poet has to struggle to perform his servitude to words and dominate them well enough so that he can reveal aspects of reality in his own way, usually not denotatively but connotatively.

In one of the poems Silva published in his lifetime, "Estrofas" (Stanzas),[53] later called "Ars" (Art) (p. 58) (with some textual changes in the manuscript later prepared by Silva), the poet expresses the idea that "El verso es vaso santo" (Verse is a sacred vessel) (p. 58). In that sacred vessel he stresses that there should be placed only "Un pensamiento puro" (A pure thought) (p. 58). This poem is from Silva's early period, and he reflects the belief that poetry writing is a sacred art and that its creation should be inspired by the most noble and delicate subjects. This gives to art a moral quality which is belied by some of the poems later written by Silva. It also stresses the balsamic, cathartic quality of poems for the writer, and his role as preserver of memories, of the essence of old things and of beauty.

In "Un Poema" (A Poem) (pp. 65–67), Silva shows his Modernist ideas of desiring to write a poem "De arte nervioso y nuevo" (Of new and nervous art) (p. 65). The poet personifies all the elements which make up a poem: rhythm, rhyme, and subjects. He uses all these to paint a scene of them circling around him as he chooses the correct ones for his inspiration. He writes a poem in which he is demonstrating his process in the making of a poem, but at the same time he creates images which appeal to all the senses, and especially the sense of sound because of his choice of words for their musical qualities. He is following the Symbolist and Modernist tendency to write poems of "vagas sugestiones" (vague suggestions) (p. 66), but the final couplet shows his disappointment and disillusionment because of lack of communication. He finds that the poet is a person who is isolated from everyone and cannot encounter understanding, since, as he says: "Le mostré mi poema a un crítico estupendo . . . /Y lo leyó seis veces y me dijo . . . ¡No entiendo!" (I showed my poem to a stupendous critic . . . /And he read it six times and he said to me, . . . I do not understand!) (p. 66).

Silva considers in this poem that the art of the poet is like embroidery with "frases de oro" (golden phrases) (p. 66). It is a composition filled with metaphors which refer to poetry, for example: "tercetos, como corceles ágiles" (tercets, like agile steeds) (p. 65), stanzas which sound like a bell with the "retintín claro de su campanilleo" (the clear ting-a-ling of the ringing) (p. 66). There are rhymes "de plata y de cristal" (of silver and of crystal) (p. 66), verses "color de amatista" (of amethyst color) (p. 67), and there is the "soneto rey" (sonnet king) (p. 66). (The latter is an example of pure metaphor by juxtaposing two nouns, a metaphor rarely used by Silva.) There are syllables "dulces como el sabor de un beso" (sweet like the taste of a kiss) (p. 66), an example of synaesthesia, and "palabras que ocultan como un velo" (words that hide like a veil) (p. 66). The latter image reflects Silva's desire to write poems which suggest rather than state.

In the poem dedicated "A Diego Fallón" (To Diego Fallón) (pp. 115–16), Silva stresses to Fallón that when his poems are forgotten (and, he implies, those which he or any other poet may write), there will still be poetry, for according to Silva, Nature will still continue to form an all-encompassing poem "que rima en una estrofa inmensa/los leves nidos y los hondos valles" (which rhymes in one immense stanza/the fragile birds' nests and the deep valleys) (p. 116).

"Avant-propos" (Prologue) (pp. 87–88) is the poem which is

usually published preceding Silva's "Gotas Amargas." First he reflects upon what the physicians prescribe when the stomach is giving problems, that one take a bitter tonic or potion. Then he urges that when the literary stomach feels ill from reading "todas las sensiblerías semi-románticas" (all the semi-Romantic mushiness) (p. 88) that the reader try "una dosis de estas/gotas amargas" (a dose of these/bitter potions) (p. 88).

In conclusion, concerning Silva's poetic theory and its reflection in his original poems, there is a polarity to be observed. He portrays the intellection of artistic production which counteracts the Romantic myth of the oracular poet, unconscious or conscious intermediary of the deeper realities. He speaks of trying to dominate words and expression, of making an effort to find the best, most personal form for each poem. But on the other hand, José Fernández, poet-protagonist, states that poems make themselves, and come out when they are ready. And many times Silva mentions the idea of the poet, maker of sacred verses, even though he is disillusioned with his own generation of poets. He believed in the sacredness of poetry and of its inspiration; that the poet was an artisan with words, that the poet should listen to all the voices of things, that only he could hear and transmit to his readers the eternal secrets communicated to him. Yet at the same time, he showed his failure to believe the poet would be understood by the majority of his readers, and this caused him a feeling of futility concerning the poetic art. He thought that half of the work of art had to live in the brain of the reader or viewer and was disillusioned and disappointed with the general intellectual and artistic level in South America.

Yet Silva did read the great masters and admitted that a poet should continue to read other poets and to carry on an interior life of intellectual meditation. He limits the influence of imitation to sensibility and preparation, and feels that the writer must be careful not to destroy his personal originality. In his consideration of sources for other poets, he said that often it was a similarity of organization and temperament rather than borrowing or imitation. Silva's poetry has often been investigated for sources, but he unites in his sensibility all the elements acquired in his wide reading. In this way, as Alfredo Roggiano testifies, he gives in his art an integration of creative temperament and values of a perfectly defined culture.[54]

Silva also showed at times a belief that poetry should serve a moral purpose or at least a social one and should not be virtriolic (in spite of his bitter poems), and not malign anyone. But one of his main preoccupations was for communication, which he made an effort to accomplish through rapid allusions in his poems. He shows his love for a subjective world rather than a too-concrete, disappointing reality which wounds and defrauds the human being, especially the poet. This is one of the characteristics which makes Silva much more contemporary than other Modernist poets of Spanish America. The reader has to think, to read between the lines, to intuit and to become contemplative to really understand his simple poems. But although simple, he still was able to enclose beauty in his poems by the selection of suggestive words of light and color, an appeal to all the senses, and use of musical values as well.

XII   *Original Poems of Miscellaneous Themes*

Among these poems included in the category of miscellanea are those which fit into too many categories, making their classification almost impossible. For example "Obra Humana" (Human Works) (p. 58) is a poem which seems to be a description of a scene in the pristine, untouched jungle in the month of May with the moon lighting up its beauty. A few months afterwards there is a railroad passing through, a railway station, and even a telegraph line. Both scenes are described using the most musical and suggestive words. But the poet does not indicate his feelings about the apparent progress, and the reader has to determine, with little evidence, whether or not Silva is exalting the epoch of the wireless and of the railroad or whether he is being critical of the destruction of the calm and unchanged jungle.

An extemporaneous poem, a toast which begins "De los rosados labios . . ." (From the rosy lips . . .),[55] is the only poem, remembered by anyone, which Silva improvised. While not an outstanding poem, the wishes he expresses for the persons at the gathering and for the hosts are couched in the simple yet musical languages which Silva used so well.

"Sinfonía Color de Fresa con Leche" (Strawberry and Cream-Colored Symphony)[56] is an ironic poem, as can be seen immediately by the title, and is dedicated "to the decadent hummingbirds." In the first stanza of this poem the author points out what he intends to do: to tell a "historia rubendariaca" (story like those told by imitators of Rubén Darío) (pp. 152–55), and it is evident that the poet means the inferior imitators of Darío. It uses to excess all the techniques which the minor poets, following Darío's lead, are apt to do, such as their choice of exotic vocabulary: "argentados cisnes" (silvery swans), "bizantino esmalte" (Byzantine enamel), "noche diáfana de plenilunio" (diaphanous night of a full moon). It uses arcane references to mythology, to little-known writers and figures of the past. It terminates with the judgment that these are the chaotic verses of the descendants of Rubén Darío's "Princesa Verde y el Paje Abril,/rubio y sutil" (Green Princess and Page April,/blonde and subtle) (p. 154).

There are many trite phrases used in this ironic poem, made trite by overuse by the Romantics, as well as by Rubén Darío and his followers and imitators. Therefore one could not choose it to go into an edition of the works of Silva except as a literary curiosity and a way of showing that Silva was well aware of the work of Rubén Darío and of the Modernist movement with its abuses and excesses. Silva was without doubt aware that he was also a Modernist, but knew that his art was a much more simple, less exotic one than that of those he calls the "Byzantine" or exotic poets who enjoy the "babel" (p. 154) of their jargon.

There are two poems by Silva concerning prayer which are somewhat surprising for an agnostic. "Oración" (Prayer)[57] is number XIV of the series entitled "Notas Perdidas." Since the first edition, it has been published in the collections of Silva's poems. It describes the innocent bedroom of a young girl. A comparison is made of the prayer which comes from the girl with rosy arms and goes toward the snowy arms of the crucifix of ivory. Perhaps its inclusion in the majority of the editions is because the poet does not make any judgment, either of faith or of doubt. It is an innocuous poem as far as moral ideas are concerned. Yet as always in the poems of Silva, choice of vocabulary shows the care that the poet took to choose the words which were most colorful, musical, and appealing to as many of the five senses as possible.

The other poem concerning prayer, which begins "¡Señor! ¡Mirad las almas..." (Lord! Look on the souls...)[58] is a plea to God for mercy for the souls who searched in human love for the eternal. It asks for the strength to go through life accepting adversities, struggling against abominable luck and dominating the corrupt flesh. The tone of this poem seems to be that of Silva's second period. If it is, rather than a renewed faith it shows that at a certain short period during the years before his suicide, the poet was hoping against hope that he might find enough faith to sustain him in those most difficult times.

XIII   *Translations*

Of the poems translated by Silva from French and English authors, three were published during Silva's lifetime, in his youthful first period; and one other was probably written around that time although not published. In the manuscript prepared for publication by Silva, he did not list these translations or versions, indicating that he did not consider them to be important. They are all from Romantic poets, and they show Silva's early inclinations and tastes, since choosing to write a version or translation means that the poet understands or feels deeply the inspiration of the writer of the original. They will be considered in chronological order and compared with the original poem.

Beginning with "Las Golondrinas" (The Swallows), by Pierre Jean Béranger,[59] one notes that Silva was seventeen years of age when this poem appeared. Although Silva did change the order of the second and third stanzas in his translation, it is fairly literal. The poem relates the laments of a prisoner of war who asks that the swallows bring him news of his country, his mother, and his valley. He questions whether or not his sister has married yet, if his companions have returned to the village, and if during his three years in chains his land has been invaded and destroyed by the enemy (pp. 105–107). The only appreciable straying from the text appears to be caused by the exigencies of the language into which he was translating, and by his choice of adjectives which show more emotion than the original.[60]

"Imitación" (Imitation)[61] is a twenty-line poem inspired by a ten-line poem by Maurice de Guérin, entitled "Fragment."[62] Although as can be observed by the doubling of the number of lines, it is elaborated much more than the original, the content and theme are essentially the same. The additional vocabulary, as in some of Silva's translations of prose, are to add color and music to the understated language used by the French poet. The theme relates to a crest of a huge rock or cliff which has cavities where the rain water accumulates. That is where the protagonist, the "yo" (I) of the poem, comes to meditate on his failure in love: "Ici je viens pleurer sur la roche d'Onelle/De mon premier amour l'illusion cruelle" (I come here to cry at the Onelle Rock/ The cruel disillusion of my first love).[63]

In the Spanish version these same two lines become four:

Yo suelo por las tardes
ir a la cima a sollozar a solas
y mi llanto se mezcla con las
    aguas
entre las piedras toscas.[64]

(I usually go in the afternoon
to the crest to cry alone
and my tears are mixed with
    the water
among the craggy rocks.)

The final lines in the French poem and the final stanza in the Spanish version warn the swallows never to drink the bitter tears left by the sad lover in the cavities of the stone. We note that Silva has preferred not to use the actual location, giving the poem more universality (pp. 125–26).

"Realidad" (Reality)[65] is again almost a literal translation of the main ideas of Victor Hugo in the original. The poet testifies that Nature is the same everywhere, even though the names of places and persons are different. He addresses the poet, urging that he tell of anything which exists, and if his spirit is pure, nothing of what he says can be evil. Hugo terminates the poem with these lines:

La vérité n'a pas de bornes.
Grâce au grand Pan, dieu
    bestial,
Fils, le réel montre ses cornes
Sur le front bleu de l'ideal.[66]

(Reality has no limitations.
Thanks to the great Pan, the
    beast-god,
My son, reality shows its horns
On the blue forehead of the Ideal.)

Silva gives these same lines in a different manner, a more suggestive, less literal way:

¡No tiene la verdad límites, hijo!	(Truth has no limits, son!
Del gran Pan, dios bestial, la hirsuta barba	Of the great god Pan, beast-god, his bristly beard
y los cuernos torcidos se columbran	and twisted horns are glimpsed
del ideal tras de la frante pálida. (pp. 107–108)	behind the pale forehead of the ideal.)

"Las voces silenciosas" (The Silent Voices)[67] has appeared in many editions, subsequent to the first, with the title "De Lord Tennyson." In this poem the ten lines in the original version in English become eighteen in Silva's Spanish, and the same techniques are used by the poet to embellish and make more musical the sounds of the poem by choice of vocabulary, and unlike Tennyson's original, by using a refrain. The poem is concerned with the silent voices of the people who have died and who in the hour of silence call the poet back to the past. He requests rather that they call him onward and upward. In this translation, Silva follows rigorously the ideas of Tennyson, but embroiders; for example, when Tennyson says "clothed in black," Silva says "vestida de fúnebras crespones" (dressed in funeral crepes).[68]

One might say that some of the changes Silva made in the texts of the originals in his translations of poems were because of the necessities of the rhythm and meter, as well as the sounds of the languages. But many of the different choices he made are necessary in translating poetry into good poetry. Of course, if a straight prose translation is given, the idea is literally the same in the other language, and the problem does not exist. But when a poet translates the poetry of another poet, it usually has to be a version if it is going to be poetic in the other language. If the effort to make it poetic comes into play, then the ideas and inspiration of the translator or version writer are reflected in the choices made. One could say with impunity that no two poets would come out with the same version of a poem, because the choices would be intimately tied to the aesthetics of the translator or version maker.

After considering all the poems of Silva found previous to 1977, in general one could say that he wrote his poems on the various themes mentioned with a suggestiveness (in his best poems) which reflects his search for integral purity. Others among the Modernists concentrated so much on an ornate vocabulary that the poems often sank beneath the weight of the images and metaphors. Silva had a rhythmic sense which, combined with the simplicity of his vocabulary, chosen for its sound and musicality as well as suggestiveness, unified his ideas and the words chosen to represent them.

CHAPTER 4

De Sobremesa: Silva's Modernist Novel

I *The Editions*

THE single novel written by José Asunción Silva, as noted in the biographical chapter, was lost in the sinking of the ship *L'Amerique*, on his return from Caracas. But when his friend Hernando Villa, who feared Silva was going to commit suicide, asked him to rewrite one of the lost manuscripts, Silva allowed his friend to choose the one he preferred. Villa chose the novel, *De Sobremesa* (After-Dinner Chat), which Silva duly rewrote in his distinctive handwriting, before his suicide.[1] However, the manuscript was not published until 1925, when the first edition was produced by Cromos of Bogotá.[2] It was a small edition, and a second edition came out in 1928[3] by the same publishing house. After that, it has been included in several editions of the complete works of Silva, such as the one by the Bank of Colombia.[4]

Even after the publication of the first edition of the complete novel in 1925, several of the interpolated essays or digressions were published separately many times in anthologies, obviously out of context. The titles of the essays were often selected by the editors. Citations from these essays were used to prove different ideas that the author could not possibly have meant.

The date of Silva's death, 1896, together with the subsequent date of publication of the first edition of *De Sobremesa* in 1925, twenty-nine years later, surely reflects the attitude of his family, which delayed the publication of the manuscript in its entirety. It was not a book which in his time would have been favorite reading. The same shock value is there which often appeared in his "Gotas Amargas" (Bitter Potions). The family did not wish the complete manuscript to be published, fearing it would hurt

94

his reputation or his family name. It was published when the times had changed enough, or Silva's worth as a poet had consecrated his name.

Even after its publication the work was mainly ignored, even though the newness of the prose style in Spanish and the subjects treated were related to those used in earlier Modernist renovation in prose. (It was similar to such novels as *A Rebours* by Joris-Karl Huysmans, published in Paris in 1884; *Il Piacere*, by Gabriele D'Annunzio, published in Milan in 1889; and *The Picture of Dorian Gray*, by Oscar Wilde, published in London in 1891.) But in Spanish America, Modernistic prose was being written in the 1870s by José Martí and Manuel Guriérrez Nájera and others, as well as by Silva, as we can see in some of his earlier essays. The first writing of *De Sobremesa*[5] probably dates from one decade later than the Modernist revolution in prose. The same currents are visible in his search for new and more aesthetic ways of writing, clothing his ideas in an original, more flexible form.

II   *The Plot*

To facilitate further reference to the novel *De Sobremesa*, a detailed summary of the novel follows. Although portraying Silva's lack of organization, the résumé seemed best in a chronological arrangement, with his interpolations summarized as they appeared.

The novel begins with a Modernist description of a luxurious interior in semidarkness: "Concentrated by the gauze and lace lampshade, the tepid light of the lamp fell in a circle upon the scarlet velvet of the carpet and illuminating entirely three china cups, glazed in the depths by a trace of strong coffee, and a cut crystal glass filled with a transparent liquor glimmering with golden particles, left hidden in the dark purple shadow produced by the tone of the carpet, the hangings and tapestries, the rest of the silent chamber."[6]

Then as the candelabra is lit, we see the poet-protagonist, José Fernández, and his friends Juan Rovira and Oscar Sáenz, who are conversing after finishing a sumptuous dinner. Sáenz explains why he is silent, awed by the luxurious contrast in his friend's house to the life to which he is accustomed, that of a poor medical doctor. He enumerates the many elements which surround him in the Fernández house, which only a rich man can have. He then points out that all his friends envy Fernández because of these things, as well as his amorous adventures.

Sáenz urges him to write more poetry and not to rest on his laurels after having published only two books of poems. He reproaches Fernández for not having written a line for two years, and for dissipating his life in many different directions at the same time. Fernández replies that he is not a poet when compared with the great poets of past ages. He also attests that one cannot write poems by force of will, that they are formed within the poet by his inspiration and come out already formed. Fernández also tells his friends that many of his poems are inspired by his reading of the great poets of the past. He discloses that he dreamed and still dreams of writing great poetry by suggesting the many obscure things he feels within. But he informs them that he cannot consecrate himself to that when he has so much curiosity and enthusiasm for living and for many other things than poetry.

Sáenz says that his isolation in a luxurious house where he has social contacts with only some ten of his friends, most of whom are also somewhat eccentric, is not the most propitious way for living real life. Fernández replies, giving a long meditation on "real life," and begins by asking. "What is real life, tell me, the bourgeois life without emotions and without curiosity?"[7]

The protagonist affirms that most of the people who are alive have not really lived, and that he is doing his best to really live in every possible way. His medical friend discloses that all the refinements should be taken away from him so that he would write poetry. Fernández tells him that the skull he keeps on his desk to remind him of death shows him that his only duty is to live life to the fullest.

Yet he explains that he is still tempted to write the verses which often seem to be formed, struggling to emerge. However, he is convinced the readers would fail to understand his poems, as did the critic who called him a pornographic poet.[8] Again he reiterates the Symbolist tenet that he does not wish to express his ideas openly, but only to suggest them in his poems. This requires readers who are artists, and unfortunately, according to Silva, the public lacks artistic understanding.

Rovira interrupts this conversation between Fernández and Dr. Sáenz and urges him to read from a book which has some connection with: 1) the name of the house Fernández is building, Villa Helena; 2) with a design of three leaves and a butterfly hovering above them; and 3) with a pre-Raphaelite painting he owns. At this moment two other friends arrive, Luis Cordovez and Máximo Pérez. Luis Cordovez begins to ask also that Fernández read to him and the others from the notes he took during a trip to Switzerland. Pérez, who is ill, chimes in and asks that he read about an illness Fernández had in Europe.

Fernández begins to meditate on Helena and attributes to her supernatural power the vision he has seen that very day of a butterfly, and then, that same evening, the four requests by his friends that he read about her. He considers that perhaps these happenings are a message from Helena on the anniversary of his discovery that she had died, a time of the year when he is always emotionally ill.

Fernández commences reading from the diary covered luxuriously with an encrustation of the emblem of a butterfly fluttering over three leaves. He wrote this subjective diary during a brief stay in Europe. The first entry is dated Paris, June 3, in the 1890s. From the first line its introspective quality is obvious. It deals with José Fernández's most intimate personality. The work has a great many interpolated essays which reflect his reactions to certain happenings, books he read, and things he heard during the European trip. The essay included later in the first part concerns the reading of two books, works which were popular in the 1890s: one is a book by Max Nordau. *Dégénéréscence*, cited by Silva from the first French edition, translated from the German and published in 1894.[9] The other is the *Journal* of Marie Bashkirtseff, published for the first time in Paris in 1887.[10] Nordau, a psychologist, judges the artists of his time according to his specialization, coming to the conclusion that they are neurotic or psychological cases. Fernández is especially incensed with Nordau's treatment of Marie Bashkirtseff, a Russian artist who died of tuberculosis in Paris on October 31, 1884.[11] In her diary we see the same desires of Fernández, carried to extremes, of living life abundantly; being, seeing, and doing everything.

Silva discusses Marie Bashkirtseff's diary, in which she recorded her experiences from the age of twelve until eleven days before her death. She describes her life of luxury and her enjoyment of it, but also her rebellion against its meaninglessness. She recounts her struggles to educate herself to a higher level, her arrogance, her romantic fancies and daydreams, as well as her ambition to live to the fullest extent, and especially to gain fame as a painter. Until her death she worked at the Académie Julian, a well-known painters' academy. She also describes her struggles with her increasing pain and suffering in the final days of her fatal illness.[12]

In his work Nordau analyzed with an implacable harshness the pre-Raphaelite painters, the work of the great composer Wagner, Verlaine, and many other writers of high literary acclaim, as well as Marie Bashkirtseff. He called them "the degenerates" but admitted in his preface that they were not all criminals. He believed that many were artists who had gained numerous admirers and were the creators of a new kind of art. But all were rebels against society.[13] His book was very popular during the 1890s, and he probably made Bashkirtseff famous by including her with the other outstanding artists.

Silva was often said to have known Marie Bashkirtseff, but he did not arrive in Paris until the same month she died. Although he speaks of the Passy Cemetery, where she is interred,[14] he knew her only literarily, and perhaps not until the year before his death, when he was writing anew De Sobremesa. He was familiar with the article "La Légende d'une cosmopolite" by Maurice Barrés, which was included in the long section, "Trois stations de Psychotérapie" (one of the works found beside Silva's bed when he committed suicide), in which Barrés characterizes Marie as "Our Lady of Perpetual Desire."[15]

The inserted critical essay by Silva-Fernández of the books by Bashkirtseff and by Nordeau, the latter work especially, shows that Silva was familiar with the literary currents of the period in France and was also aware of the great furor caused among the so-called decadent writers by the German psychologist's work. Silva was familiar with these artists, who were often considered to be decadent, because of an attitude which Silva shared, a predominantly aesthetic attitude toward art.

After this critical digression in which the author displays his literary knowledge, the protagonist, Fernández, talks about his own life. He tells of years of constant action and of passion for the luxuries of life, as well as a desire for social prominence in his native country. He describes the growth of his infinite curiosity concerning evil and complains of having tired of operating in his country, which he considers limited, with its vulgar women and its business with little challenge. These factors inspire him to leave the country and to act the part of the rich South American snob in Europe, hunting with the noblemen, dancing cotillions, and spending time in tailors' establishments. But, on the other hand, Fernández describes his opposite side. He is the collector of eighty oil paintings, four hundred watercolors and etchings, medals, bronze, marble, and porcelain pieces, tapestries, outstanding editions of his favorite authors, on special paper, bound luxuriously to his order. He is a student of science who frequents the Sorbonne to hear lectures, a speculator in the stock market, a gourmet, horseback rider, lover of magnificent women, of fine furniture, of wines thirty years old, and, above all, an analyst of himself who believes he sees clearly all the multiple impulses of his psyche.

Yet in spite of all these activities, Fernández discloses that the intense life he is living does not satisfy him, that perhaps of more worth is the laborer, or the anarchist executed for throwing a bomb, since at least he had a plan and a purpose to which he dedicated his life. But such a plan according to the protagonist is very different from the useless plans he elaborates, for example a house of commerce established in New York, a trip around the world, or a pearl-fishing trip.

An entry of June 23, in Bâle, Switzerland, gives a hint of what happened the previous day. There was a violent scene and he had to flee. He implies that by now the woman must have died, and the police probably are looking for him, although he has registered under a false name and identity. He communicates to his readers that he is to go to Whyl, Switzerland, to wait for a telegram from Marinoni, his financial adviser.

The entry dated June 29, in Whyl, discloses the contents of the telegram from Marinoni. It informs him that the girl involved, Lelia Orloff, has been seen in public and that apparently nothing serious had happened to her. Fernández does not understand how there was not a sign of a wound since he knows there was blood on his shirtsleeve.

The following day's entry explains the violence, but is lugubriously coupled with the news of the death of Fernández's grandmother, the last relative he had in the world. The letter telling of her agony describes her prayers for Fernández and repeats her last words of thanks that Fernández has been saved, by the "sign of the cross by the hand of a virgin, the bouquet of roses which falls in his night like a sign of salvation."[16]

The impression caused by his proximity to committing murder and the death of his grandmother shocks him. Then the details are given of the cause of his murderous attack with a knife on Lelia Orloff, his beautiful mistress of the past several months. From the beginning she showed a natural taste for the most luxurious in refined furnishings and possessions, and like him she needed the most profound and exquisite sensations. Her natural aristocratic bearing and tastes caused her to be very attractive to Fernández, and when he first notices that Angela de Roberto was her occasional visitor, he protested. Later, on arriving unexpectedly and learning that the two women are in the bedroom together, he reacts violently, and after breaking down the door he describes the scene, saying "I threw the infamous group to the floor on the black bearskin which is at the foot of the bed, and began striking them furiously with all my strength, stimulating screams and blasphemies, with violent hands, with my boot heels, as someone who smashes a snake. I do not know how I took out of its leather sheath the little Damasquined Toledan knife, engraved like a jewel, which I always carry with me, and I plunged it into her soft flesh twice; I felt my hand soaked with warm blood. . . ."[17]

After feeling the blood, Fernández flees, leaving her screaming. He hurries to the office of Miranda, another of his financial advisers. After getting some money and his correspondence, he goes to his hotel, where his old servant Francisco packs his luggage so that Fernández can take the first train out of the city, to Bâle, Switzerland. As always, the hero analyzes his reactions, and in this case cannot understand his violence since he is never intellectually shocked by the abnormal. In fact, he points out that the abnormal has always fascinated him as a proof of the rebellion of man against instinct. He feels it was a stupid incident, comparing it to a senseless duel he provoked for no good reason with a German diplomat.

Affected emotionally by all these events, Fernández decides to stay out in the country in a small house of an old couple to be able to think. He has sent to Paris for the books and other articles he needs, and meanwhile is going to study prehistoric America and botany. He is living quite primitively since he was unable to eat the food they prepared for him and is drinking only milk. He is surrounded by simplicity in their house and is following a regimen of mountain climbing, study, and meditation. He views nature as a kind of nirvana in which he enters. He compares the sesation with one he felt in the crossing of the ocean, when the exterior spectacle seemed to enter into his being, and he felt a pantheistic ecstasy and union with nature. He only lacks the ecstasy in the Swiss mountains. These two instances are the only times the protagonist considers nature.

Fernández feels a supreme peace in the mountains after his previous months of dissipation. He has meditated until he has come upon a plan to double or triple his fortune by selling the gold mines inherited from his father. Then he will transfer the funds to New York and found the business he had thought of starting with Carillo, who is backed by the Astors. Fernández will try to learn all he can about the fabulous development of the United States, and from New York will go occasionally to Panama to direct the pearl-fishing in person. Then, with all the capital earned, he will proceed to put into effect his political plan.

The plan which Silva puts into the mouth of his protagonist is an ultraconservative, dictatorial theory of government to enable the young, rich South American to improve his underdeveloped country. But the vision is not so implausible, since it mirrors the actual mode of government for many South American countries. The plan centers on the protagonist himself, who is to ascertain first the needs of the people through a tour of the provinces, accompanied by selected engineers and scholars. After entering into a minor political post where he engages in two years of investigation and study of governmental administration, Fernández develops a financial plan which will solve all the problems of the coutry. He obtains a ministry office, and using his influence gained in that office, he directs the formation of a new political party of "civilized men" who believe in science and education, and are far from religious or political fanaticism. Fernández becomes the president, through an effective publicity campaign, and in that office continues to work for improvements in public education, agriculture, mining, commerce, and industry, while promoting immigration to form a new and powerful race. Finally, after long, peaceful evolution of the established government, Fernández retires, leaving the power in the hands of "competent persons."

The protagonist discusses an alternative in case the utopian plan does not succeed through peaceful means. The people must be incited to a conservative reaction against false liberalism. The clergy must instigate the masses to arise. And a tyranny, later becoming a dictatorship, must be established through military power. A new constitution is promulgated, and revolts are kept down by the muzzling of the press, the exile of powerful opposition figures, and through confiscation of the property of the enemies of the government. With proper economic measures taken by the dictatorship with Fernández at its head, in a few years the country will be rich and peaceful. While it is impossible to be sure that Silva was considering these plans as a serious solution, even as fictional plans for his hero they show a naiveté concerning the simplicity of a government's operation, and one cannot fail to notice his lack of political ideological depth.

Fernández dreams of the success of these measures in bringing progress to his country. He visualizes the transformation of the capital to a delightful place as the Paris of Baron Haussmann. He hopes that the progress will not only be reflected in a material way, but in art, in the sciences, in a national novel, in poetry which celebrates the indigenous legends, the glorious wars of emancipation, the natural beauty, and the splendid future of the regenerated land.

He points out the incongruity of establishing a conservative dictatorship like that of Gabriel García Moreno in Ecuador or of Manuel Estrada Cabrera in Guatemala in order to bring about the sweeping changes he encompasses in his plan. But he attests that the country is tired of demagogues and of false liberties in constitutions which do not function. He feels that the people prefer the cry of a dictator who follows through on his threats, rather than that of a more platonic promise of respect for law, which is never carried out.[18]

Fernández sees himself in that faraway future retiring finally from his position as dictator to write poetry containing the supreme elixir of his many experiences—poetry of mystic tone, and apocalyptic, very different from that written when he was twenty, full of lust and fire. His last years seem peaceful and replete with philosophical pursuits, but he prognosticates that "Over my still-tepid corpse, a legend will begin to form which will make me appear as a monstrous problem of psychological complication to the generations of the future."[19]

Here he is talking about having been a dictator, and the mixed emotions that the people would undoubtedly have felt toward him. These lines are often cited as Silva's feeling about himself, yet it can be observed clearly that they are concerned solely with his fictional protagonist in his planned role as dictator.

At a break in the reading of the diary, Fernández says to his guests that he must have been mad while writing that plan. Sáenz says that it was the only time he had been lucid. Rovira tells him that being president of the republic would be degrading for Fernández. Asked if the financial part of his plan had been successful, Fernández replies that the earnings were more than expected. But when asked why he did not carry through with his plans, the doctor answers for him, saying it was because of the pleasures of life. Juan Rovira leaves, disclosing that while he loves to hear Fernández read his prose production, he does not understand anything of what he has heard. When Cordovez insists that Fernández return to his reading of the diary, Fernández begins with an entry from Interlaken, July 25. Again Fernández praises the effects of nature on man as a calmative agent and as a purification of those who retire to meditate, taking away all sensuous desires which abound in the city. With these ideas in mind Fernández thinks of the seductiveness of Lelia

Orloff and laughs aloud as he savors his freedom from desire for her and for the sensual life.

The following day, July 26, Fernández continues in the same vein with a long tirade against life in the city and against the common people with their atrocious tastes unlike those of refined aristocrats such as he.

On August 5, Fernández's fifty days of abstinence are broken by Nini Rousset, a vulgar actress who had previously disdained him in Paris. She arrives at his hotel in Interlaken and seeing his name on the register comes to visit him and remains with him for the night for an orgy. Fernández detests her, but cannot resist her, even though for him she is the incarnation of all the Parisian vices.

On August 9, in Geneva, Fernández awakens after forty-eight hours under the influence of opium. He took the opium in revulsion after the night spent with Nini Rousset in his room, in order to escape from his memory of trying to choke Nini, probably because she had undone his rational and chaste plan of abstinence. She fled crying, half-dressed, from his room, and Fernández took a huge dose of opium to escape. The combination of the orgy, drinking, and the opium leaves him in a miserable physical condition when he comes to himself.

In Geneva, August 11, Fernández is having dinner in a small dining room when a young girl and her father enter. The young girl looks to Fernández like a painting of a picture by Van Dyck; her hands are like those of Anne of Austria in the painting of Rubens, and Fernández is unable to take his eyes from her. He feels that the attraction is mutual, but he is ashamed of his past life as he faces her in her innocence. He feels in her glance a compassionate tenderness resulting in peace of mind for him. He is overexcited and his imagination creates an intense understanding without ever speaking a word to the blue-eyed beauty. He hears them speaking Italian and they mention St. Moritz, among other places. Then they leave the dining room to have their after-dinner coffee served in their room. As they depart, Fernández meets her eyes again, and she seems like a supernatural being with an earthly beauty. Fernández finds on the floor a cameo which has a branch with three leaves and a butterfly fluttering above it with its wings open. He keeps the cameo to return it to her the next day and is pleased, since he thinks that it will enable him to make her acquaintance. Helena's appearance is never clarified, although isolated features are mentiond; her blue eyes, graceful carriage, and dignified poise. She shares with the Romantic and Modernist heroines such characteristics as her extreme youth, sixteen or seventeen years, her status as an orphan who had lost her mother at the age of four, her apparent physical frailty and seeming inclination to be consumptive, as was her mother.

Fernández learns that they had arrived a few hours earlier from Nice, and the Count Robert de Scilly had said that he and his daughter Helena de Scilly Dancourt, would remain two days. They did not give the name of a place where they were going. Fernández is glad that he has never had a love affair with a girl whose name was Helena.

An old friend, Enrique Lorenzana, comes to visit him and is surprised to see that Fernández looks so horribly disfigured and pale. He convinces Fernández to accompany him to a lecture on history. On walking back to the hotel in the moonlight, with the stars shining above, Fernández thinks of Helena and enters the garden of the hotel to continue his solitary walk. He looks up and sees one of the balconies on the second floor with the window open. A tall slender shadow of a woman can be seen against the gauze curtains. Fernández picks some flowers, puts his card with them, and throws them up through the window curtains into the room. Helena comes out, reminding him of a painting by Fra Angelico, and raising her hand she makes the sign of the cross as she throws him a bunch of white flowers. Fernández seems to hear the words of his dying grandmother and he nearly faints. When he recovers, all he has are the flowers, and the lights have gone out in her room.

Fernández cannot sleep without the aid of two grams of chloral hydrate, and he dreams of all the day's images, awakening at ten in the morning. He bathes, and when he is served breakfast he asks the waiter to find out if Count Scilly and his daughter have gone out. Fernández learns that they left very early in a private coach and the concierge did not hear to which station they directed the driver to take them.

Now the desperate search for the ideal, the chaste Helena,

begins. Fernández has fallen in love with her, and he begins an anguished search for her as his last chance for salvation. He has only seen her twice and has dreamed of her more than actually seeing her clearly. She represents a creature of light, and he feels that she alone is capable of saving and redeeming him. The reader knows from the beginning of the novel that Fernández will never find her, but her person never dies in his soul, and in homage to his pure love for her he is constructing a villa in Colombia which is named for her. He has difficulty in beginning his search since he has no idea where she was going. He preserves the bunch of white roses in a crystal box to take with him. He has received a letter saying that the buyer of the gold mines has agreed on the price and he must be in London on the fifteenth of the month to sign the papers. He plans to go to all the places he heard Helena and her father mention in the dining room, as soon as he finishes his business with his English bankers.

Painting is one of the main themes in *De Sobremesa*, since it creates imaginatively the dreams of the protagonist. Helena, who belonged to the family of Rossetti, a painter of the pre-Raphaelite school, is a shadow which the protagonist forms into a painting from the first time he sees her. Later, when he owns the painting of Helena's mother, the wife of the count, Helena becomes even more of an icon for him. Fernández searches for her and for her father all through Europe, finding her only in the grave, leaving him with his ideal intact but without solutions for his emotional future. From the beginning her beauty causes him to remember museum pieces, and in his first encounter with her we see the Modernist techniques of the fusion of painting and fiction.

In the entry of October 11, in London, Fernández mentions that during the two months spent in London finishing up his business deal he has taken the time to send telegrams to all the major European hotels asking about the count and his daughter, and has written letters to travel agencies trying to find them. At night he evokes her figure as he reads the poetry of Shelley and Rossetti and sometimes he calls her name and seems to see her come toward him without touching the floor. He thinks of her in terms of purity and innocence, and the phrases he uses are the verses of Dante concerning Beatrice. He meditates upon the seventy days spent chastely in London, without mixing with the society he knows would have welcomed him. His friend Enrique Lorenzana, who came to see him in Geneva after his bout with opium, sees him in London and tells him that he looks like another person. Fernández has the sensation that this is true, but wishes that he did not have the incurable nostalgia for the blue eyes of the love he has lost.

In the London entry for September 10, Fernández is preparing himself in the daytime, for development of his country, studying armaments and military maneuvers for when they will be necessary. He is still buying works of art, such as watercolors and paintings, but is experiencing no strong emotions. Nevertheless he has horrible nightmares when he again sees the three leaves on the branch and the butterfly fluttering above them. He feels that his love for Helena is like an obsession. When she appears to him he always things of the Latin phrase "Manibus date lilia plenis" (Give handfuls of lilies).

Fernández knows that although all this is wonderfully sentimental and ideal, he needs physiological fulfillment with some of his old mistresses. But none of them is in London. And he is revolted by the idea of buying caresses, feeling such a practice to be nearly impossible for him.

The entry for November 13 describes how an assignation is arranged by his friend Roberto Blundel with a beautiful woman, Constanza Lundseer. But Fernández is unable to consummate the union because of a vision of his grandmother and of Helena, and because of a bunch of white tea roses (which Constanza has received from Nice) from which a butterfly escapes, fluttering above the flowers. Another coincidence is that the flowers are tied with the same cross-shaped ribbon as the ones which Helena tossed him. Fernández flees superstitiously from the union, hoping desperately that he can find Helena soon.

Still in London, on November 17, Fernández has talked with his Greek professor about his friend Dr. John Rivington, who has studied the pessimistic attitudes of humans and other works of experimental psychology and psychophysics. Fernández has already read the books of Rivington, and finally goes to consult with him, carrying two letters of introduction. Fernández says

that he is an atheist but he is coming to the scientist with faith
in his properties as a corporal and spiritual director. Rivington
asks Fernández to tell him his life history, about the antecedents
of his family, his life in his own country, the city in which he
was raised, the present organization of his life, his plans for the
future, and his present occupations. He tells the doctor of his
monastic existence since his meeting with Helena, the plans he
is elaborating concerning his country, and the incident of his
sexual failure in the bedroom of Constanza Landseer. Asked by
the doctor if he intends to marry Helena if he finds her, Fernández becomes confused, showing his shock at the idea. Dr.
Rivington urges Fernández to make all his body functions a
regular habit, and not to go to extremes with anything, to regularize his sexual necessities so as not to confuse them with his feelings toward Helena.

Rivington tells him to search for the girl and marry her and
not to make her into a supernatural being because of the coincidence of some words said by his dying grandmother which
seemed to foretell the meeting with Helena. Then Rivington
begins to question Fernández about the description of Helena
and finally asks him if he wishes to see his vision in a painting.
Rivington takes him to see a pre-Raphaelite painting he owns
which is so like Helena that Fernández feels sure it is a likeness
of Helena. The doctor tells him it is a likeness of Helena's
mother. He questions him about his visit to London ten years
earlier and whether or not he has ever viewed paintings like
this one in museums. Rivington feels that Fernández might have
imagined a good part of his feelings toward Helena after seeing
such a painting in his youth. Rivington advises Fernández to live
a more normal life, to concentrate on less ambitious undertak-
ings, and to search for Helena, the girl he wishes to marry. He
diagnoses in Fernández a double inheritance from his ancestors;
on the one hand ascetic tendencies, and on the other a desire for
a wild and active life of sexual and other kinds of excitement.
He advises him to leave all drug usage such as morphine, opium,
or ether, because he has a predisposition for drugs and thus could
easily become an addict.

Fernández blames part of the duality of his personality on his
intellectual cultivation without an orderly method which, accord-

ing to him, destroyed his faith and gave him an ardent curiosity to experience all the possible activities in life, both good and evil. He analyzes the feelings of terror which come to those who have intellectually denied God, and yet he fears that some of the teachings of his childhood might be true. He considers the terror of madness, sometimes induced by taking drugs, and even considers moments of deep depression, when he has felt that death by his own hand would be the only solution, but is lacking the energy to perform the act. Returning to the theme of madness he points out that he, just as many others, has felt its nearness. And he questions why it should be so disgraceful to go mad if such great artists as Baudelaire and others of equal stature have gone mad. But then he thinks of Helena, who is going to save him from all of these things he has mentioned and give him absolution.

Once again there is a break from the reading of the diary when Sáenz breaks in and tells Fernández that he has not lived the life advised by Rivington for the last eight years. Fernández says that his life is different now because he has distributed his energies equally amongst pleasure, study, and action. Also he has left off having violent, emotional affairs with women because he scorns all women, and for that reason has two affairs at once so that they counterbalance each other. Once again Fernández continues when Máximo Pérez asks his friend to resume his reading.

In the entry from London, November 20, Fernández analyzes himself and the contradictory inheritance from the side of his family which was ascetic and the side of his family which was violently active, both of which make him so changeable in his impulses. He relates the death of his mother when he was ten and his internship in a Jesuit school, from which he was then sent to the ranch of the Monteverdes, his cousins, where he lived the brutal life of the rich "patrón" (ranch-owner). The Monteverdes alternated between all types of violent activities and sexual orgies in which Fernández also took part. He feels that all these factors are the causes of his alternating between epochs of savage action, and of meditation, when he enters into a state of ascetic continence.

In the entry dated December 5, London, Fernández begins

to investigate the pre-Raphaelite painters, which he admits is an example of his impracticality. But, in a long disquisition, Fernández elaborates on the idea that practical persons are inferior to the impractical ones like himself. He decides to make a return visit to Rivington and goes to his office. There in the waiting room Fernández becomes upset by the psychologically ill persons waiting to see the doctor. When he enters the office he begins to cry, and asks the doctor to assure him that he is not crazy like the people in the waiting room. He also asks the doctor to have a copy made of the painting of Helena's mother. The doctor urges Fernández to search for the girl and dream no longer. Fernández decides to go to Paris to seek her. He thinks of all the things he has done in London, studying Greek and Russian, the arts of war, agronomy, and also his studies and viewings of art, especially the pre-Raphaelite. He also enumerates all the various things of value that he has collected during his stay.

Rivington only has partial success and admits it to Fernández. Finally, Fernández recurs to Charvet, actually a pseudonym invented by Silva for Charcot, precursor of Freud. His malady is diagnosed as neurasthenic ailments. The protagonist is ironical concerning the fancy medical terms which the psychiatric practitioners use, but nevertheless, he is cured twice from the nervous collapses he falls into.[20]

Psychotherapy is discussed at great length in Rivington's office concerning the problems of Fernández. His diagnosis seems to be a neurosis attributed in part to his contradictory inheritance, with one side of the family fanatically religious, inhibited persons, and with wild, orgiastic, antireligious persons on the other. Also, Rivington suggests that some of the protagonist's problems have resulted because he was an orphan, losing his mother when he was ten years of age, and other family members at a relatively early age, leaving him without relatives at the death of his grandmother.

With such fluctuation in his emotional states, where drugs, mysticism, and sexual orgies alternate with periods of sexual abstinence, Fernández apparently has mental aberrations. These problems cause numerous allusions to psychotherapy in the novel. It is a theme used as subject for some of the essayistic digressions, such as those on madness.[21]

On December 26 the entry explains that, once again emotionally ill, Fernández consults with Charvet. When Charvet hears of his five months of sexual abstinence, he says that Fernández should not follow such capricious behavior. But on learning that the protagonist is stubbornly bent on such behavior, he prescribes violent exercises, long hot baths, and large doses of bromides. But the suggestions give no results, and the protagonist continues to feel a violent depression. On December 27, Fernández is somewhat better, but then he becomes worse again and stays in bed for a few days. His servant, Francisco, goes to see Fernández's friends the Mirandas, who bring two doctors to diagnose his illness. The friends gossip while the doctors consider his case. Silva is very ironical in this passage, making a long enumeration of all the neuroses and psychological terms for illness which the two doctors use. They finally prescribe a purgative for Fernández, which he does not intend to take. Then his friend Marinoni says that he will go for Dr. Charvet, who comes that evening. Fernández asks for drugs to allow him to escape the horrible, anguished feeling he has. Dr. Charvet finally prescribes a medicine which has a positive effect, and within a few days Fernández is able to get out of bed. But the doctor warns him that he can have a relapse which might prostrate him at any time.

On New Year's Eve, Fernández goes out but soon begins to feel ill again. In front of a shop window, which has a great marble clock, he begins to experience all the terrors he felt before and finally loses consciousness in front of the window. He becomes conscious again in his own bed with Marinoni and Francisco his servant, accompanying him. Fernández says that he is saved, even though he has a horrible headache, since the anguished feeling which has tormented him has disappeared. In bed that night in a feverish condition, nevertheless, he is improving, and in succeeding days he finally regains his health. Charvet tells him again to enjoy life, but not excessively, and to marry and be happy.

On March 10, Rivington sends Fernández a copy of the painting of the mother of Helena, and the protagonist makes a kind of chapel, with the painting of Helena's mother on one wall and the picture of his grandmother painted for him by James McNeill Whistler on the other wall. Below the painting of Helena's mother is a bronze table he keeps filled with several different varieties of flowers ordered by telegram from Cannes. He has a chair there on which to meditate and read, a box where he keeps the jewels he has bought for her and the cameo Helena droppd in the restaurant. He also has a crystal box in which is preserved the bunch of flowers she tossed to him.

On March 10 Charvet, in one of his consultations with Fernández, sees the picture and mentions that Scilly Dancourt is an acquaintance of his. Charvet tells Fernández that Helena's mother died of tuberculosis while he was attending her, and the husband, who had a daughter four years of age, was deeply affected by his wife's death. Charvet tells Fernández the name of the only other person he knows who corresponds with Scilly, General des Zardes.

On March 20, Fernández goes to see the general. He does not know anything about Scilly at that moment, but tells Fernández that a Professor Mortha has contact with him. On seeing Mortha, Fernández is told that the only connection he has with Scilly is by mail through his bankers, Lazard, Casseres and Company. They are also financially connected with Fernández, and he goes there to investigate. He learns that they know little, but that the last check of Count Scilly was cashed in Alexandria.

Fernández meditates on April 12 on what little he has learned from his investigations except about the life of the father, previously a military man who on the death of his wife has turned to a study of religions, traveling through the world with his daughter. Fernández discloses that he has sentimentally rented for ten years the room where Helena slept in that Swiss inn, and he maintains it closed, as well as the room in the house back in his native land where his grandmother died.

On April 13 there is a long digression about what he would like to do for Helena if he were to find her. He would build her a castle and he sentimentally describes what he feels would be the reaction of the country people to her beauty: "There will be sunny mornings in which they will see us pass riding on horseback on a pair of Arabian horses over the roads which extend through the plain, and the rough country people will kneel upon seeing you, thinking you are an angel, when you look at their bodies deformed by their rustic chores with your shining blue eyes. . . ."[22]

Dated April 14 is one of the long essays in which Fernández treats of various themes such as: Ibsen, the Russians, Nietzsche, neo-Mysticism, and the theosophical centers of Paris. Sometimes one does not really understand whether Fernández is being serious about what he discusses or whether he is speaking ironically; for example, the long analysis of the trends of the epoch, where it is difficult to see whether Fernández is on the side of the anarchists or not. At times one seems to see an obvious irony, and at other times one could interpret his thoughts and ideas as his serious opinions; for example, in the following lines: "Thus with explosions of dynamite in the foundations of the palaces and striking down the most profound moral foundations, which were the older beliefs, humanity marches toward the ideal reign of justice. . . ."[23]

Another passage in which Fernández is talking about the religions of the present and especially about the Buddhists gives the reader the same doubtful feeling as to whether or not the author believed in what he was saying: "Do you still doubt concerning the Renaissance of Idealism and neo-Mysticism, you, spirit which questions the future and sees the old religions collapsing?. . . Look: from the obscure land of the Orient, the home of the gods, Buddhism and magic are returning to conquer the Western world. Paris, the Metropolis, opens to them its doors as Rome opened its doors to the cults of Mitra and Isis: there are fifty theosophical centers, hundreds of societies which investigate the mysterious psychological phenomena; Tolstoy abandons his art to publicize in a practical way charity and altruism; mankind is redeemed; the new faith lights her torches to shed light on her shadowy way."[24]

Although it is not possible to cite all the passages which would give a clearer view of Fernández's often quite perceptive ideas about the spirit of the present, this section reflects deep thought and meditation.

On April 15, the entry contains more of his evocations of the profound love he feels for Helena. The section of the diary dated April 19, however, is very different in tone from the previous evocation. Fernández enters a jewelry store, which provokes a favo-

rite technique of the Modernists, a word picture of all the gems
he sees, as well as all those which he can imagine. The following
citation is only a small part of the world's gems which he paints:
"Oh, sparkling stones, splendid and invulnerable, you vivid gems
which slept for entire centuries in the depths of the earth, delight
to the eye, symbol and summary of human riches. The diamonds
shine with iridescence like drops of light. . . ."[25]

While Fernández is in the jewelry store, a girl with a Yankee
accent comes in, and when she asks about a diamond necklace,
she indicates that it is too expensive. Fernández offers it to her
but she refuses; however, they make a date for nine that evening.
After she leaves, Fernández buys the necklace to take to her
as a gift. When he gives her the necklace that evening, she
offers to pay for it since it is the one that she has asked her
millionaire husband to buy for her without convincing him.
Only after she learns he is the famous poet José Fernández does
she soften and permit him to give her the necklace, thus opening
the door to her seduction, not in her hotel but in his. She told
him she was leaving the next day for New York, and Fernández
knew that this would be his only night with Nelly, the wife of a
Yankee millionaire.

Five months later, on the first of September, Fernández remembers the night with Nelly as having been only a droplet
incapable of satisfying his horrible thirst. He gives a party and
seduces three different girls, but none of them is really what he
wants. He is searching for his lost love, Helena, and the caresses of these girls leave him with a feeling of bitterness and
scorn for everything. He comments on the empty heavens
because of his lack of faith. He is sure his thirst for the supreme,
the absolute, is part of what causes his dissatisfaction.

His friend Rivas asks Fernández to stay with his wife, Consuelo, while he and three other friends spend the evening with
four females whom he calls "horizontals." Fernández brings
Consuelo flowers from his greenhouse, orchids the same as grown
in Colombia and which in their youth they had looked at
together. In those long-ago times, Consuelo and Fernández
had felt fondness for each other before her marriage to Rivas.
Fernández tells her that he has always loved her and asks her
pardon. She, in turn, tells him he is her only love. Fernández

asks her to meet him the next day, which she does, and their love affair begins.

Another conquest, the blonde German baroness, is seduced by the use of other wiles; Fernández playing hard to get and cool toward her. He challenges her to kiss him, and to meet with him the next afternoon. She tells him that what fascinates her in him is his scorn for the current morality. Julia Musellaro, an Italian girl, also seduced by Fernández, has libertinous conversations in her house, where she receives her guests every Tuesday evening. Fernández invites her to come to see him on Thursday morning, when they can be as pagan as they like. Fernández considers that he is perhaps behaving as a Don Juan, except in the case of Consuelo, his childhood sweetheart. He feels that he does not seduce anyone, that the seduction is mutual because of a common desire for pleasure and adventure. He meets the Italian girl later, and she has what he feels is a false story to tell him about a piece of jewelry that a "friend" needs to sell. He tells her to have it sent to him and he will send her a check.

Rivas continues sending his wife to Fernández, urging Consuelo to go sightseeing in Paris with their friend, and seems not to feel the least bit worried about his wife. Consuelo tells Fernández that everyone, including her husband, calls him "el casto José" (the chaste José).[26] Although Consuelo had been ill, she begins to improve with the affection of José and making love to him every day. For three months their idyll continues, then Rivas and his wife leave for San Sebastian, and although they invite José to accompany them, he declines. Rivas thanks Fernández for the time spent with his wife, which has resulted in her great improvement in health. In his short observations dated September 18, Fernández indicates that he does not wish to accompany them and that if they return he intends to tell Rivas that his wife should not be trusted to spend her evenings with him.

His personal record of October 1 recounts a conversation with Camilo Monteverde, first cousin of Fernández, who is considered by the protagonist to be ignorant in the subject of art, and for that reason they hardly ever talk of such themes together. His cousin's philosophy of life is to praise others' possessions highly in order that they be given to him as gifts. He lives as easily as he can without studying or working very much and says that although both are from the Andrade tree, Fernández is like Don Quixote while he on the contrary is like Sancho. In this section, as was pointed out by Bernardo Gicovate, for the first time in Spanish, Silva write a burlesque of Ramón de Campoamor, using him as an example of intellectual mediocrity. Fernández is convinced that Monteverde has absolutely no taste in poetry because his favorite poet is Campoamor.[27] It should be remembered that Silva has often been compared to Campoamor in some of his "Gotas Amargas." It is obvious that the poet-protagonist of *De Sobremesa* was not seriously impressed with Campoamor's poetic talents, and that whatever respect Silva had felt for him probably no longer existed.

In his observations dated October 15, Fernández remembers Helena strongly again and returns to his meditation in the room of the paintings after an absence of several days. The flowers that had been placed there last were dead, and the room smelled of death. Fernández decided to move the things to other parts of his living quarters, and to put the paintings in his bedroom.

The diary for October 25 describes another period of searching for Helena, sending telegrams and spending ten days in investigation, with no success.

The diary now jumps to January 16, where it is revealed that Fernández has been unconscious for ten days, and again Charvet has had to be consulted. Between life and death for a few days, Fernández finally recovers and decides to leave for America to try to forget his failure to find Helena through immersing himself in mercantile operations. He returns to a cemetery where he has spent several afternoons, and there sees the emblem he has come to connect with Helena, the three leaves and the butterfly. He nearly faints, and catches himself by a column. His friend Marinoni comes to his aid, and as Fernández starts to lose consciousness in the arms of Marinoni, he sees the inscription of Helena's name and the date of her death. He mourns her death and says that perhaps she never truly existed, but that she was his dream and was more real than what men call reality. Her early death prevents the consummation of the love Fernández feels for her, and she can then enter completely the realm of the ideal, without loss of chastity, in word or deed, becoming the perfect object for the protagonist's adoration. Fernández ends the reading of the diary and closes the book. His friends remain silent and Silva gives a last artistic description of the luxurious interior as though it were a painting.

III *General Critical Commentary on the Plot, Scenes, and Characters*

De Sobremesa lacks a well-designed and constructed plot, as most critics who have studied the novel have noted. For example, Arias Argáez cites Sanín Cano as having said that *De Sobremesa* was a work of defective construction, of arbitrary analysis and of purely subjective truth.[28] Yet there are paragraphs in which Silva shows some talent as a storyteller and also reveals his stylistic command of the Spanish language. *De Sobremesa* is a series of short narrations dated as entries in a diary. It includes incidents and episodes as well as digressions which in reality are essays. This interpolation of essays makes the novel seem rather unorganized and hard to summarize and to follow except for the unification of the plot provided by the hero of the work, José Fernández.

As the plot summary indicates, the diary relates the European trip of a rich South American, José Fernández, poet and art collector, who is beleaguered with psychological problems. He glimpses fleetingly a mysterious child-woman with whom he falls in love at first sight. He tells of the search, a kind of pilgrimage all across Europe in search of this ideal love whom he finds only in the grave.

The hero appears at times to be a stylized reflection of Silva. The character, however, is Silva and is not Silva, as in all autobiographical novels, where usually the author uses much of his own knowledge about many men, and not solely about himself. Sometimes the reader does not know whether or not Silva is referring to his own feelings or fictional ones. Nevertheless, this has not deterred many critics from quoting the majority of the words Silva puts into the mouth of his protagonist as his own thoughts and aspirations. Yet at times the character is a very different one from Silva, who at the moment of rewriting the novel was undoubtedly already decided concerning his suicide.

There can be no doubt about the reasons an author chooses to write a novel using an autobiographical approach. In this way it is possible to objectify his own contradictory psychology, and the novel is an exploration of the psychology of an artist. Since Fernández is a prose writer and poet, we are able to observe his ideas about writing poetry, ideas elaborated on by the author and put into the mouth of the hero. The narrative mode, the auto-biographical novel, is one which reveals more fully the char-acter of the hero, yet it gives a unilateral approach to the consciousness of a person, and such is the intimate diary read in a long after-dinner session with friends. Since the actual after-dinner chat is cut to such a minimum, perhaps it would have been better to entitle it *The Reading of My Diary*. The novel is so long that it does not seem plausible that it could be read at one sitting, but such acceptance of the illogical has been one of the concomitants of most types of art.

Silva wanted to write a psychological novel which would reveal the complicated psyche and soul of the artist, in this case a particular artist who showed a duality in his alternation between sexual orgies and periods of abstinence, when he would search for the ideal. When reading the summary of this un-usually frank book for Silva's epoch in Colombia, it is easy to understand why his novel was not published until twenty-nine years after his death. As Juan Loveluck has said, the novel presents a kind of nonsystematic analysis of the man of the end of the nineteenth century and his basic conflicts in the world.[29] But the presentation was of a man as artist and aesthete, whose problems were often different from those of the majority of men of those years. The narration does reflect the consuming intellectual interests of the time when the pre-Freudians were beginning to elaborate their theories. The protagonist's interests are made manifest in psychology, psychopathology, and para-psychology, as well as the mental explorations which the author probably knew about personally, in Paris, when Charcot and other pre-Freudian psychological investigators were extremely popular.

In the case of Silva-Fernández, the artist (or other man), who is unable to find the sensitive spirit he craves in a woman, comes to feel completely frustrated, as if there were no being in existence who might meet him on his own footing. Then he creates an ideal of femininity, even though he must occasionally break loose and try to gain release by union with female flesh. Nevertheless, he has such revulsion for himself after these orgies that he destroys what little physiological relief he might have gained. Yet he must prove he is a man every day.

Fernández's ideal of perfect womanhood was Helena, an adolescent whom he sees only at a distance and does not know well enough to do anything but idealize her. The whole novel is in part a search for Helena, with the characteristics of a detective story in the investigation of clues to her whereabouts. But the search is fruitless and she becomes for Fernández the mystery woman, later his impossible love, and finally his muse. This idealization of Helena does not help the protagonist to have a more normal attitude toward women, nor does it prevent the sexual affairs which cause his self-revulsion. And, even though he does not leave off drugs or his encounters with other women, his self-hatred afterwards indicates that these were only substitutes for the ideal who lives solely in his memory. A less blunt and truthful writer would have left these amorous adventures out of the work, but Silva is illustrating the teaching of his day, the double standard which was ingrained in the young men from the beginning.

Often this novel has had very adverse criticism and a close study of it over many years does not cause it to gain in stature in the mind of this student of Silva's works. Yet it can be compared favorably with Modernist novels such as *Idolos Rotos* (Broken Idols) of Manuel Díaz Rodríquez, and others of the time. Perhaps it is not as good as the author would have liked it to be since it was reconstructed in the most terrible years which Silva suffered. He rewrote it after he had lost all the import business along with his capital and a great part of his personal property, after he had tried without success to make a career in diplomacy, after a shipwreck in which he lost much of his unpublished work, and after he had failed once again in starting the tile factory in Bogotá. He was, at the time, a complete failure, unable to find a way to maintain his mother and sister. Unemployed, he did rewrite this novel requested by his friend Fernando Villa before taking the suicide route out of all his problems. The mere fact of rewriting a long novel from memory without any notes means that it could not have the same consistency and organization of the manuscript lost in the ship *L'Amerique*. For that reason it is probably more equitable to characterize his prose writings in some of his short essays written at a much earlier time, as will be done in the next chapter.

The scenes where the novel takes place give us a cosmopolitan view of the world. It begins with the luxurious salon, where the reading of the intimate diary of a world traveler, a rich South American, takes place. The interior of the room where the protagonist reads his journal aloud, and chats with his friends, is in a South American city which is not identified, but it is probably Bogotá or perhaps Caracas. It is a novel, however, of taking a trip, an idea so dear to the mind of the young people of most epochs, especially today—taking a trip in every sense of the word. Most of the other scenes are in bedrooms where Fernández's conquests take place or in the interiors of luxurious houses, with the one exception of the few days when Fernández stays in the house of the Swiss couple. And only there, during his stay in the mountains, does the hero describe any scenes of nature. This indicates that nature did not enter into Silva's prose as an important element.

The setting is usually urban as in most of the Modernist novels. The characters also are urban. They are mostly rich, artistically knowledgeable, international, usually bilingual or trilingual, reflecting a universal culture. They are often expatriates from several different countries. Some of the characters are mature psychologists or psychiatric physicians. They are all adults or young adults. The youngest character is Helena, who is a teen-ager when the hero glimpses her. The protagonist is twenty-seven years old. The only child even mentioned in the novel is Helena, as a child of four when she lost her mother. This indicates that Silva was not concerned with a realistic portrayal of life, but with a psychological portrayal of the psyche of an artist. And he succeeds admirably, in spite of the disorganization apparent in the work.

IV *Autobiographical Elements*

The element of fiction which is always present should not be confused, as some critics have done, apparently believing that the character created by the writer and the writer himself in his historical person are one and the same. However, Silva did use the fictional character to reflect some of the same tortures he suffered. He depicts the suffering of a young man who could not adapt to the conservative and rigid society into which he was born and whose problems were exacerbated because he was an artist who could not adapt to the society in which he found himself.

It can be said that Silva drew upon his personal experiences, and those things also that he dreamed of doing but could never afford. Some of those elements which are autobiographical are the fact that both were poets, and that Fernández expresses many of the same ideas concerning poetic theory and other subjects which Silva made clear in essays and poems. But there are differences: no ideal love is known to have played a part of any importance in Silva's life. He was never anywhere near being a millionaire, nor did he have enough money to live the luxurious life the hero lives, as for example buying a magnificent diamond necklace for Nelly to enable him to seduce her and remain with her one night.

The work is in a way a complement of the biography of Silva in that it analyzes the crisis of a poet much like himself, and the intellectual surroundings he found in Europe in those days. It is a work which also demonstrates the wide knowledge of the author in art and in literature, as well as other fields such as neuropsychology. It also shows some of his mistaken ideas, as for example the idea that thirty-year-old wines would of necessity be good ones,[30] or that the artistocracy of Europe could trace their ancestry back to Roman times.[31] There is no doubt that Silva did identify himself often with his protagonist, but it is a mistake to exaggerate out of proportion the auto-biographical descriptions in the work, attributing them all to Silva, and not to the protagonist he has created out of his imagination.

One of the many ways in which Fernández is a reflection of

Silva is in his dissatisfaction with his surroundings, with the bourgeois atmosphere which both the author and the protagonist reject as being mediocre, vile, and philistinian. Fernández is critical of the public, with its lack of understanding.[32] He expresses his hatred of the bourgeois life without emotions and without curiosity.[33] He is scornful of Latin American politics, manifested by the plan he elaborates to make sweeping changes.[34] He is scornful of the admirers of mediocrity,[35] of vulgar mercantile work and all the institutions of a life which is empty without the sanctuary of art.[36] Some of the other themes toward which the protagonist shows a critical attitude, probably similar to that of Silva, were: religion,[37] reality,[38] socialists,[39] the Jews,[40] the United States,[41] and even the visual pollution of Niagara Falls.[42]

Silva himself had many psychological problems, often resulting from real tragedies in his life, which were a contributing factor in his suicide. But his protagonist in the novel had many that were different from Silva's, mostly as a result of his alternating abstinence and sexual excesses, as well as his search for the ideal which was never fulfilled. Silva had to concentrate on earning a living and had little time to search for the ideal.

One suspects that the friends who listen to the reading of the diary, and those whom he meets in Paris and London and the other places Fernández visits, are taken from real-life models. However, all the women, with the exception of Consuelo, who is delineated as a live person from his native country, seem to have come from the author's wide reading, or his imagination. They lack reality, since there is little difference to be observed among them, or among his feelings for them.

More than simply mirroring Silva, the protagonist delineates the spiritual disorientation of those years, reflected by most of the Modernist writers. Fernández is a walking compedium of all the weaknesses and vacillations the Modernist artists had in resolving their lives in those days.

Like Des Esseintes in *A Rebours,* by Joris-Karl Huysmans, Fernández in many ways was the double of the author, and both writers were braving the stigma attached to the autobiographical novel, uniting the mystery of creation and autobiography. But not only in being both the creator and in part the created one does Silva show us his duality; his chosen protagonist is partly an aesthete and partly an unsatisfied man, tormented by his financial and personal difficulties. Silva therefore is behind Fernández and often comes forth with more force than the protagonist. De Sobremesa is a book halfway between pure autobiography and pure fiction, sometimes both at the same time, other times one or the other. De Sobremesa is, on the most profound level, pure autobiography; that is, on the basis of the aspirations of the soul and of the thirst for the absolute of the hero, Fernández. It does not matter that the autobiographical details of Fernández are not completely those of Silva, since the literary and artistic traits seem to blend.

Like Silva, Fernández is the author of books of poetry, two in the case of the protagonist, one in the case of the author, but Silva lost some manuscripts of poems in the wreck of the ship L'Amerique. The early poems of Fernández are said to be erotic, and are denigrated by him compared with the great creations found in the poetry of the past.

Fernández gives his theory of poetry, and it is a clear idea of Symbolist poetry, and perhaps it is the theory of Silva as well, since he has stated several times in poems essentially the same thing: "It is that I do not want to state, but to suggest, and in order for the suggestion to be produced, it is necessary that the reader be an artist. In imaginations deprived of faculties of this type, what effect can a work of art produce? None. Half of it is in the verse, statue, or painting, the other half in the head of the one who hears, sees, or dreams."[43]

According to a friend of Silva, Juan Evangelista Manrique,[44] the words of the protagonist of De Sobremesa concerning his education could be applied to Silva to describe his intellectual development: "An intellectual education undertaken without method and with crazy pretentions to universality, an intellectual cultivation which has ended up in the loss of all faith, in the burlesque of all human barriers, in an ardent curiosity for evil, in the desire to carry out all life's experiences, completed the work of other influences. . . ."[45]

Silva always desired the luxuries which surrounded him in his childhood, and after entering into the world of business, burdened with the debts inherited from his father, he was unable to obtain them in the quantity he might have wished. He reflected his lack of fulfillment of these desires by having his protagonist enjoy all of them.

The hero is profoundly interested in his own health, in his physical and mental hygiene, and this reflects the preoccupation of Silva himself during his last days when he had hypochondriac moments. But in Silva's life the sexual excesses were not possible. These preoccupations were undoubtedly wishful thinking on the part of Silva or aggrandizement of the normal pattern of Latin American youths of visiting brothels in those days. By giving so much sexual prowess to his protagonist, Silva is able to counteract in a once-removed way the reputation he himself (as well as Fernández) had gained as being the chaste, virginal young man, without experience in sexual encounters.

Some of the doctors who attend Fernández are based on real-life characters, as Charvet, and perhaps others. Charvet, as mentioned, was the veiled identity of Charcot, a pre-Freudian psychologist. The detailed description of Fernández's illness seems to be imaginary; however, Silva was always interested in reading any kind of manual, especially in psychology or psychiatry. It is true that Silva himself visited in Europe and was at many of the places where his entries are dated, but his life could not have been that of the millionaire protagonist. He must have moved in entirely different circles, if he was lucky enough to move in any circles at all in European society, except for that of the expatriates.

The European setting reflects Silva's trip to Europe, but actually little is known about what he did there except to visit Juan Evangelista Manrique, who was a medical student in Paris. Manrique testifies that Silva tried to learn all he could from him and from the persons he talked to by going to all the lectures he could attend, and by reading all the latest books. Nevertheless, it is dangerous, in the author's opinion, to equate unequivocally Silva and José Fernández since undoubtedly Silva alternates real happenings with fictional elements and modifies many of the factual elements.

V *Romantic Elements*

One of the most constantly used characteristics of the Romantic novel is vagueness, and concerning Helena the protagonist assigns an unknown or exotic origin to the heroine, revealing the truth only gradually. Fernández is vague about names and identities, and often one has to search for the name or the identity of the characters who are his friends, or girls to whom he is making love.

In some Romantic novels, symbols and mythology are used frequently. In *De Sobremesa* they are used somewhat differently than in Romantic works in that there is an element of foreboding and terror associated with the ideal attachment which will inevitably be frustrated, as is known from the beginning of *De Sobremesa*. The supernatural symbols in the novel are connected with the words of the grandmother on her death, the throwing of a bunch of flowers by Helena to Fernández from her window, the finding of her brooch with three leaves and a hovering butterfly, and the appearance of butterflies at crucial moments. Silva uses other techniques related to the Romantics such as premonition, and open anticipation of the tragic ending.

The Romantic elements in *De Sobremesa* are mainly in tone, an exacerbated consciousness of his scorn for life. And the Modernists added to the uncovering of the sentimental life a profound literary self-consciousness concerning style and form which modify profoundly the Romantic sentimentality.

The subtle use of augury in the work gives the reader the idea of impending tragedy of the death of Helena. But it is also Modernist in the use of the emblem of the butterfly as a supernatural indication of Helena's presence, and as an indication of Fernández's belief in the supernatural. It is evident that this use of augury is to increase in the reader the anguished hope that Fernández will find Helena, but in a way, for some more observant readers, it is known from early on in the book what the outcome will be, and the interest of the reader shifts to how the actions will be accomplished.

Considering that one of the characteristics most commonly connected with Romanticism was that of an uncurbed revelation of the most intimate self, the protagonist fits that characteristic as much as any of the heroes of the Romantic novels. The "yo" (I) of the hero is the most important thing in the work and is the main theme of the novel.

The emphasis on religion, which was one of the Romantic tendencies, is present in *De Sobremesa* but in a negative way, in the lack of religion of the protagonist. Yet he is obsessed by doubts concerning his agnostic or atheistic beliefs, and thinks always of his grandmother's prayer for him when she was dying.

Probably one of the main characteristics which seems Romantic and goes against the sensibilities of the twentieth-century reader of *De Sobremesa* is the sentimental dwelling on his sorrows. Fernández even says he prefers to suffer. He has a tendency to dwell on his own grief in an overly emotional way.

In general, Romantic literature represents a reality which destroys love; and a life without love, for the protagonist, has little meaning. Such is the case with Fernández and Helena, even though Fernández is not able to remain faithful to her physiologically. For Fernández, as for the Romantic hero, the noblest type of love is that which remains unfulfilled. The impossible love was one of the most common themes preferred in Romanticism. It became popular probably because of the belief that marriage brings out the imperfect in love, and for that reason Fernández is so shocked when he is told by Dr. Rivington that, of course, he will marry the girl. His love for her was more pleasing to him when posited from an idealizing distance. This attitude has resulted from the medieval traditions of courtly love, when marriage was not the desired state for a lover to feel an ideal passion for the beloved.

From the medieval courtly love tradition also comes the belief that the lovers who suffer the most are the most fulfilled. The suffering of Fernández is in a more modern manner with his various sexual affairs with other women. He certainly is not trying to immortalize Helena by his faithfulness, but perhaps this is a reflection of his modernity, where man no longer has the idea that he can only be happy with one woman.

Also, the preservation of the flowers thrown to him by Helena is somehow overly Romantic for the sensibilities of the present, and dates the work; but just because it reflects a taste not the same as is presently common does not mean that only in his time were such sentiments commonly felt and expressed.

Although Fernández does not compare his Helena or other lovers with blossoms or other aspects of nature as did the Romantics, there is a strong presence of flowers in the novel. The emblematic use of the three leaves and the butterfly has already been noted: Helena is identified with the bouquet of white roses she threw to Fernández, which he tries to preserve for as long as possible in a crystal box. The connection between Fernández and Consuelo is also related to flowers, orchids.

One of the most typical Romantic elements in *De Sobremesa* is the concept of love as entertained by the protagonist. The attachment is intense and spiritualized since their encounters have always been in shadows and without real communication except in symbolic gestures which, it is insinuated, might have been misinterpreted by the hero. The intensity and longevity of his attachment for Helena is reflected in his guarding zealously the bouquet of white tea roses, and also Fernández's desire to obtain a copy of the painting of Helena's mother, who was so like the daughter. His chapel, where he placed her painting and other emblems and relics, indicates these same ideas.

Although Silva rarely describes nature, in the few descriptions he does poeticize what he observes. Unlike the Romanticists, Silva does not use nature as a vehicle of his emotions. The observer does not reflect or parallel nature in his state of mind. Yet the scene in which Silva describes the ocean is a favorite scene of the Romantics, in which the hero sits alone contemplating the light of the moon. In Silva's novel it is not with melancholy feelings but in harmony with the Modernist idea that nature was the only place where the artist could expand and become part of the universe. Silva thus uses nature in two ways. One, by showing a pantheistic union with it, and the other by the Rousseauian idea of the return to pure and peaceful nature, contrasted with the vices of city life.

Also Romantic was the use of the theme of death. From the beginning it is known that the death of Helena is to terminate Fernández's search for her. This was a common Romantic approach: the story of the love of a beautiful, idealized girl ended by her death.

One of the characteristics which was Romantic as well as Modernist was Silva's preoccupation with the search for the source of the artistic inspiration, a theme returned to again and again.

VI *Modernist Tendencies*

In the work *De Sobremesa* there is a deep and constant reflection of a preoccupation with the new art of portraiture being painted in Europe during those years: pre-Raphaelite art. The ideal Helena of Fernández's dreams is the image of one of the paintings, and Silva adds to this emphasis by having the character descend from the family of the wife of Rossetti, one of the pre-Raphaelite painters. Fernández finally finds a portrait in the pre-Raphaelite style, not of Helena, but of her mother, who resembles her, painted shortly before her early death from tuberculosis. There is a spiritualization of Helena similar to the kind utilized in the art of the pre-Raphaelites. She is so spiritualized that she is often unreal, even in the mind of the protagonist.

In Modernist novels like *De Sobremesa,* the heroes were non-conformists and did not adapt to their society. They fought the practical businessman (even when they were as successful in business as José Fernández), and the battle was not ignored by the enemy, since they knew that the members of society looked for practical success and did not care in the least for the successes of art. Silva, however, was forced to live in both camps, at least until the liquidation of the bankruptcy, and even then had to search, without much success, for a Maecenas, a political sinecure that would allow him to live in his artistic world.

In Modernist fiction the heroes were generally "Los Raros" (the strange ones), as Rubén Darío called them, and the "neurotics," as they were called by Max Nordau. However, these heroes were idealized by the other artists in their own intellectualized atmosphere and often were obsessed by art as the only world where they could exist. The Modernists had inherited much of the Romantic tradition in these elements; for example, the cult of the sacred artist, and protest at the lack of comprehension in a vulgar and practical society which tended to frustrate the artist completely. They were often considered economic outcasts unless they could find a friend with influence who would either obtain for them a diplomatic post or give them a stipend on which to live.

The Modernist novel might seem to be a very different novel from what is normally considered to be Spanish-American. However, the novel of Modernism many times had as subject the psychological analysis of the victims of bitterness, the rebels in society, the neuropathic artists, made neuropathic by society, the persons usually of an intense refinement and hyperaesthetic sensibility. Because of this interest in such themes, the novel of Joris-Karl Huysmans, *A Rebours,* and his protagonist Des Esseintes were popular and well known among the Modernist fiction writers.

Rebellious individualism was a characteristic of Modernism, and the fact that Silva chose to rewrite this particular novel for publication after he had lost most of his manuscripts in the sinking of the ship *L'Amérique,* shows his rebellion. It was a work that would have been too disagreeable to the sensibilities of the Colombians to publish right after his death. Also, considering that when he rewrote it, he was probably already contemplating suicide, only a rebel would have chosen to redo such a shocking book, as it must have been for his times.

De Sobremesa's construction and organization were certainly not the optimum, as many critics have pointed out, and it is somewhat difficult to read in its entirety, but it is original in the analysis of the protagonist, José Fernández. The novel shows Silva's striving for a unique way of expressing his ideas in a unique style.

God is not mentioned except in a rather insolent fashion or in a deeply doubtful concern referring to His existence. However, in the consciousness of Fernández there are bits and pieces of dead religions, and a concern with religious art, and perhaps religion thus serves as one of the main themes in the novel. Fernández makes the effort to establish a new mysticism and a new mythology with his Helena, reflecting a belief in a reality which common man did not understand and perhaps the artist was doomed never to find in this life. But art might serve as a way, a kind of religion, or perhaps an aesthetic philosophy by which the poet or artist could guide his life. Silva's disquisitions on the metaphysical implications he sees around him show only an intuitive understanding without his being able to form a system or come to any order in his beliefs.

Silva shows a basically aesthetical attitude due to his concept of artistic activity as being its own end, worthy in itself and with no need for justifying it. Therefore, his prose shows that it is a literature of the senses; it vibrates with sensual elements, and it is dazzling in its display of color. It often reads like poetry in prose, and Silva always seems to be searching for sonorous turns of phrases. Also, the history of art is almost always present, and serves as one of the inspirations, perhaps equal to Silva's own intimate experiences and thoughts. Thus he used established art works for source material in his new creation, adding more artistic qualities.

Silva's protagonist showed the typically Modernist bitterness toward mediocrity. Concerning intelligence, his attitude is that it is an aristocracy to which few, like himself, belong. For him art is noble, so noble that he feels unworthy to be named in the same breath with Shakespeare and other great artists.

The author takes refuge in distance in space, in Europe rather than South America, through his protagonist, freeing himself from his own tragic life. He then chooses from among the elements around him those which represent the most aristocratic and aesthetic world; none of the conquests of his hero is less than a famous beauty. Fernández is constantly acquiring some art object, and he tries to maintain an exquisite fictional ambience around him.

The Modernist characteristic of cosmopolitanism in *De Sobremesa* is visible in several ways. In the first place, the novel has as its scene various cosmopolitan places in Europe and, although the author describes all of them, no single one seems to attract him more than any other. He speaks very few times about the beauties of nature around him, and when he does it is solely comparing them to the unfortunate aspects of the life in a large city. But these attitudes are only displayed when he is tired of the life of dissipation he leads in the city. He projects in his protagonist the desire to assimilate the ways and values of the various European societies, to become a cosmopolitan citizen of all countries. He is always engaged in the study of different and unusual subjects both in Europe and in his homeland. This reflects an interest in subjects form many different countries. The novel itself, as Silva was rewriting it, manifests his desire to participate in the community of the elite, the aesthetically initiated. In this demonstration of the aristocratic nature of Silva's tastes and ambitions, he is the same as his protagonist. He reflects a world of books and of art, which is one of the most constantly recurring themes of the work. The protagonist cultivated collections of precious objects, whole museums of art, impressionistic refinements, antibourgeois philosophies, moral crises, and miniatures of poetic prose.

One of the impulses which aimed toward personal expression of extreme individualism was an extension and modification of a Romantic tenet, but it can be distinguished in its Modernistic modality by the peculiarly literary orientation and the artistic intensity. The Modernists were often said to be uninvolved with society, but this attitude has been discounted in the present since these writers, with their intense individuality and search for the self, contributed a great deal to the understanding of man himself and of his psyche.

Silva is trying to understand one single "I," that of his protagonist, José Fernández, and exhibits a deep philosophical pessimism, considering that man's beliefs until that moment had been only illusion. According to Silva, unchangeable principles and fundamental ideals were no longer considered a standard part of man's life. The only reality, the only truth, the only irreducible core of reality was the "I." Sensibility is one of the main elements in the philosophical ideas expressed by Silva's protagonist in *De Sobremesa,* and he negates the rational worth of the ideas that unite human beings. He denies many times the social worth of literature, making it a sublime and holy sport of the select and not understood by others, even the critics.

Modernist and Romantic tendencies and elements are combined with compatible characteristics. There are only a few lingering elements of Romanticism. One of the stylistic traits which marks Silva as a Modernist most clearly is a concern for a more subtle language and a use of vocabulary which is dissimilar to that of the Romantics. Silva's diction is ornamental, often sumptuous, and he uses the techniques of word pictures or portraits. He attempts to borrow pictorial equivalents, from watercolor, oil, pastel, or etching, and emphasizes stylistic experimentation. Concerning content, Silva forms a hero of art, showing us that the heroic concept of life is not dead, but that social and political circumstances in America have changed so much, the writers could no longer be heroes of action.

VII *Decadent Characteristics*

Bernardo Gicovate has studied *De Sobremesa* as a testimony or portrait of the European decadence which was in style during the years when Silva rewrote his novel.[46] The work *De Sobremesa* can be considered to be similiar to decadent novels such as *A Rebours*[47] (*Against the Grain*), by Joris-Karl Huysmans, in style as well as, to a certain extent, in the plot.

In style, Silva's work is like *A Rebours*, following the definition of the novel in which the whole is subordinated to the parts, rather than a classic style, where the opposite would be the case. Silva was predominantly interested in detail, and for that reason, perhaps, his novel seems more disorganized than it really is, because of the often overwhelming mass of minutiae given to us.

But Huysmans was a master of irony in *A Rebours* and always got his point across without leaving his reader confused as to whether he was being ironic or serious, as is sometimes the case in Silva's novel. However, if it is considered that the aesthetic attitude toward art is a decadent point of view, such a tendency can be observed many times in *De Sobremesa* just as in *A Rebours*. The use of words to give the effect of painting, and also the mention of many different paintings used as a part of the work, are utilized in Silva's novel as well as Huysmans's.

Yet the decadent spirit did not arise solely with the novel by Huysmans since it was visible in the Romantic period as well in different ways. For one thing, the Romantic as well as the decadent view of Christian religion was through an artistic, aesthetic prism which watered down its message to that of a mystic beauty and used its imagery in nonreligious or antireligious modes. In *De Sobremesa* this is visible, as is another trait, the feeling of loss and of desperation which became more pronounced the further the protagonist got from believing that God existed. And the neurosis of the hero added to the loss of an unaccustomed psychological dimension.

The idea of evasion to another period in time is observed in *De Sobremesa*. Even more pronounced in the decadent novels such as *A Rebours* is the flight to another epoch.

The correspondence established between literature and the other plastic arts is present in *De Sobremesa* and is also clearly obvious in novels like *A Rebours*. This is mainly used as a means of choice of words which are colorful and which reflect the contours and outlines of the things described.

The words in *De Sobremesa* seem to be chosen, as in *A Rebours*, less because of their meaning than for their power of evocation, their musical and plastic qualities. Silva wished to suggest rather than name specifically in his poetry. But in his prose the same desire is also visible.

Similar to the Duke des Esseintes is José Fernández in his neuroses. Yet in other ways Silva's protagonist was more Romantic in character and less sophisticated. Des Esseintes was a more refined and more anguished character than Fernández.

Silva, like Huysmans, reflects a striving for the virtues of individualism in any possible way, as observed in the prose poem on all the different kinds of precious stones, inserted in the episode when Fernández visits a jewelry store. Silva did not follow frequently the practice of inventing neologisms, but he did arrange the syntax of the Spanish language, already more flexible than the French, in original ways.

VIII   *Love and Women*

Although searching for Helena almost from the beginning of the novel and worshiping her image, Fernández relapses several times from his self-imposed state of chastity and has various love affairs with women. These adventures might reflect the physiological problems of a young man with normal sexual urges who decides *contra natura* to be chaste while searching for his ideal love. They might also represent Silva's erotic fan-

tasies, since Fernández has relations with seven women in the
novel: Lelia Orloff, a Lesbian; Nini Rousset; Constanza Landseer,
an Englishwoman with whom Fernández fails to consummate
the union because of a reminder of Helena in a crucial moment;
Nelly, the wife of a millionaire from Chicago; Consuelo, his
compatriot; a German baroness; and a passionate Italian, Julia
Musellaro. The friends of Fernández envy these conquests, as
his friend Rovira says: "... Your amorous adventures ... we all
envy them in secret."[48]

These conquests live in his memory only because they are
names to add to his list, like that of Don Juan. Because of the
envy of his friends and acquaintances, he is especially proud that
one night when he gives a party he is able to add three to his
list, although he does not pretend to try to understand them. He
does them favors in turn for the physiological release he can
obtain from sexual relations with them. The dichotomy is clear
in the case of Fernández: on the one hand the misogyny, the
hatred of those women who give him the release he needs, and
on the other the idealization of the one who could never dis-
appoint him in sexual relations because of her chastity and her
death before having experienced such relations.

Silva reflects a lack of knowledge about sexual relations, and
indeed about human relations between the sexes. He discloses
to us that the aristocratic Lelia Orloff is of plebeian origins,
and wonders how a common background could have produced
such an exquisite creature. He portrays her with little intellectual
capacity but an immense desire to enjoy life. Then when the
protagonist encounters Angela de Roberto visiting Lelia, he is
angry, does not like her, and when he inquires why she is there
is told bluntly that she is a friend. Then when he discovers
them in a Lesbian union, his reaction is scorn, hatred, hitting out
at Lelia and her friend with his hands and booted feet, and
trying to stab her. His actions indicate that he felt possessive
about her and did not want to share her with anyone. But aside
from his possessiveness, and in spite of what he calls his fascina-
tion for the abnormal, he shows a deep-seated aversion to that
relationship between them. Lelia as a character in a novel is a
closed personality; she is not understood by Fernández or by
the reader, and this reflects that basically Fernández felt scorn

for the women he seduced, implying the same attitude on the part of the author toward a woman he might use as a sexual object.

All the seven conquests made by Fernández are either professional prostitutes or adulteresses who acquiesce easily to Fernández's charms, thus providing him with little challenge. The accounts of his nights with these women seem strangely the same and are not always very convincing: "Of that night I only remember her smiling beauty below the full, velvet curtains of my bed, in the bedroom scarcely lit by the Byzantine lamp of dark red crystal; the impression of the strong freshness and the perfume of her adolescent body and the murmur of her voice begging me to go to the United States."[49]

One of the reasons might have been that during his time it was not customary to describe sexual relations explicitly, but in other descriptions, such as the use of drugs, he was more clear. The usual dimly lit interiors indicate shame concerning the most natural of human actions, sexual union.

The oversimplicity of treatment of women by his protagonist shows that Silva was not truly acquainted with many women in his life, except for his mother and his sisters. The other women he came into contact with were stereotyped as either beings of sheer sexuality or idealized women of purity on a pedestal. He had not had the opportunity to react to an authentic, loving woman who could combine tenderness and ideal love with sensuality, and would have had difficulty adjusting to such a woman due to the dichotomy between these two in his personality.

Perhaps the heightened sensibilities aroused by the more common acceptance at the present time of woman, as well as man, as a human being with similar rights and privileges, makes the novel *De Sobremesa* seem so anachronistic. That men should scorn the personality of a particular woman who does not happen to be a virgin, making her into less of a person, into an object of scorn, is not so common in some cultures today. His double standard is not easily accepted now, although it is still in force in Colombia to a certain extent. It takes two to engage in sexual relations, and the masculine partner is no longer considered as coming out of the relationship with his virtue intact, leaving the stain solely on the female. Even in the case of the countrywoman of Fernández, Consuelo, in spite of the fact that long ago he did feel a chaste love for her, finally he scorns her. He says that if he sees her again he will close the door in her face, and will remind her husband that it is dangerous to leave his wife with a single man, even though he be called "el casto José."

Looking from another point of view at the idea of women, there is the Romantic conception that the virtuous and chaste woman can save a man and make him into a more noble character. But then as in the present, the changing of a person is not always successful, nor does the effort always provide a happy and contented relationship.

In Silva's time men often took the position that it was sinful to feel any physical desire toward the women they intended to marry, and for that reason, on Fernández's being asked if he intended to marry Helena, he is shocked because his passion contains mainly ideal sentiments and only a minimum of sensual elements. This medieval conception, which still exists in Colombia and in other countries of Latin America, is that carnal love is considered to be divorced from spiritual love. This leads to the conduct of the hero in the novel where he seduces the women who offer him little resistance, in order to ease his physiological urges. Fernández shows a basic scorn toward these women, just as though they were prostitutes, and in fact Silva may have satisfied his physiological urges in brothels, making it impossible for him to think of finding a combination of physical and spiritual love in the same person.

Fernández was a misogynist, to use a term which is milder than some which might be used today. He felt scorn toward a woman of flesh and blood, of passions and faults. He wanted an ideal woman he could put upon a pedestal to worship. This halo of faultlessness around Helena makes her lack vitality and appear to be only the painting, which is the image, not of her, but of her mother. While he physiologically needs the seven women who are his paramours, he does not even feel humanly grateful that they are giving him at least this release. The women appear as types, types reflecting the author's and protagonist's conditioning, that of the "macho" (he-man) who must prove his sexual prowess daily. Yet while proving his sexual capabilities, when they acquiesce and accept his sexual advances, he hates them for giving in to his urgings. These are the author's fantasies of rich and beautiful women, but they are still probably based on the brothel women with whom he had the most experience. Both Silva and his protagonist, Fernández, believed in absolute male superiority with both ideal and brothel women inferior to the male.

IX   *Language and Style*

The problem of Silva and the other Modernist novelists is how to arrive at a happy medium between the plot and action of a novel and the desire of the aesthete to write an artistically elaborated prose. Several times in the novel *De Sobremesa* germs of some of the poems Silva wrote earlier or later with the same turns of phrase are visible. But these lyrical sections which are like brilliant poems in prose do not assure the creation of a good, solidly constructed novel. However, Silva is a fine prose writer with a musical style and fills his prose with cultural experiences. Paintings form the most constant motif in the novel, for there are the scenes the author paints, then there are the persons who are similar to paintings of the past. He incorporates painting in his novel in several ways: art within art, but also he shows an obvious tendency to have his novel move from painting to painting, from scene to scene, filled with chromatic refinements. Fernández lives in galleries of paintings, and reflects the eternal mania of turning everything, even the plastic arts, into literature. At the beginning of the novel there is a long pictorical description of the typical Modernist salon. Other techniques he uses are the mentioning of different schools of paintings, and of different paintings, such as those by Rembrandt, Fra Angelico, Sodoma, and painters of the pre-Raphaelite school. This technique ennobles and gives prestige, revealing a vast knowledge of museums. This method is used in the description of persons and creates an aristocratic beauty. Silva also uses movement to create a ritualistic atmosphere, as when Helena appears, combining the descriptions of slow and deliberate movements with her likeness to paintings.

The descriptions of the luxurious and sumptuous rooms which abound in the novel are chosen to give the sensation of the exquisite tastes of the artistically educated poet-protagonist. In addition to stylistic considerations, this reflects the compensation of the author, who was escaping his own bitter reality of failure, and was living vicariously in his protagonist some of his own best dreams. But his hero is rich and is able to enjoy the perversions and decadence of those who have all the money necessary to buy what they want. The novel presents the characters and the typical mansions of European decadence. One of the fundamental stylistic tenets of the Modernist novel was to create an original prose, and incorporate at the same time into the narrative literature a new hero, inherited from the Romantics, with an aura of the gods: the artist, set in the proper intellectual atmosphere. They adored another divinity as well, that of the aristocracy of the intelligence.

Silva's writing was uneven in *De Sobremesa* perhaps because it was rewritten from memory. Some of his terms are unusually colorful, but are what might be called "rubendariacos," using the terms he coined.[50] His irony at the expense of some of the characters is not comical but rather bitter, and some readers resent the author's parodies of his friends. Some of his long enumerations are boring, as for example when two medical doctors who are consulting concerning his case talk of some thirty ailments and cannot come to a common diagnosis except to give him a prescription for a purgative. Silva is inclined to give such voluminous pluralities chosen by his intuition, often felicitously, to create and give more depth to his ambience. Silva was not a bad writer of dialogue, except that speeches are sometimes longer than plausible when friends are conversing.

One other technique which adds to the poetic feeling of his prose was the use of apostrophe to give more stress to emotions. Also, he uses refrains in some poetic passages, at times repeating the same passage and at other times changing the wording slightly.

Silva reflects in the content what the writers of that period felt the novel to be, a work that does not give the reader a pleasant time, but causes him to have to think in order to penetrate into another human being, and thus perhaps to understand the universe better. Alfonso Reyes has spoken of the complex of the jungle in the Spanish-American novel, but the only jungle in *De Sobremesa* is the jungle of the complicated psyche of the protagonist, the jungle of the experiences of a man and of an artist.

Some of the most obvious elements in the Modernist style of Silva are the greater degree of intellectualism, the profound revelations of the consciousness of the ego, the sentimental projection of the principal characters as in the Romantic period but with Modernist differences. Above all, Silva reflects the profound desire to write in a new, artistic, more poetic, flexible prose, a more idealistic than realistic novel, leaving behind the nature settings which were favorites of the Romantics, and choosing cosmopolitan settings.

CHAPTER 5

Brief Prose Works

S ILVA'S brief prose works consist of short lyrical prose compositions, essays on writers, introductions to literary works and letters. Rather than give a catalog of each of these compositions before beginning and then discussing them individually, subheadings will be used to simplify their identification. In addition, two letters will be discussed in this work, one a lyrical open letter to an artist friend and the other a letter to the editor of a newspaper.

I *Lyrical Prose, "Trasposiciones" (Transpositions), "Artículos de Costumbres" (Articles about Customs)*

Although one would not think of a protest as being lyrical, "La Protesta de la Musa" (The Protest of the Muse) carries the subtitle "Prosas Líricas (Lyric Prose). It is composed as a lyrical argument by the Muse against a poet who has been wasting his time writing ironic, burlesque poems. Silva published this short article to end a literary polemic against a writer who had published a bitter satire describing several people of Bogotá, and in the bitterness which followed, many hate poems and letters were written. The writer of these satiric poems, entitled *Retratos Instantaneos* (Instantaneous Portraits), Francisco de Paula Carrasquilla, was forced to leave Bogotá, but the violent reactions and insults directed toward him did not cease. Silva was inspired to write the protest in spite of often writing satirical poetry himself. He shows his ideas about this type of poetry in the refusal of the Muse to come to aid the writer when he satirizes the errors and weaknesses of those around him. The Muse tells the poet that this is profanation of a precious talent which is sacred and should not be used on insults. The mission of the poet is to open the doors to Truth

140

and Virtue. Poetry is a noble art and the Muse abandons the unworthy poet, leaving him sobbing over his book of satirical poetry.[1] This corroborates what many of Silva's friends have said concerning the satirical poems he wrote but did not intend to publish, entitled "Gotas Amargas" (Bitter Potions). Nevertheless, in his other poems, even though he believed that ironic inspiration was unworthy, some irony appears.

"Al Carbon" (Charcoal Sketch) is one of the two which were included under the heading "Trasposiciones." It is a vignette of a scene: a still life with a donkey. In the description of the scene Silva uses various techniques for transferring the feeling of a painting to a word picture. Then he enumerates a long list of useless things in a junk room contiguous to a smoke-darkened kitchen. Silva focuses on an old donkey in the shadowy light which filters in, outlining in variegated tones, from gray to black, all the different objects in the room.[2] On finishing, one has the mental image of a charcoal sketch done by an artist who has created beauty from a combination of ugly objects.

In "Al Pastel" (Watercolor), the second of the two "Trasposiciones," Silva describes a more picturesque scene which depicts the results of a forfeit game in which the losers are given absurd penalties. The center of the word picture he paints is a fifteen-year-old girl, rather vulgarly but colorfully dressed. As a penalty, her face is painted with burnt cork, and when she rubs too hard to remove it, her skin becomes scarlet from the friction. Later her face and hair are doused with flour. She retires from the game to rest and the author uses words to paint her portrait. He sees her as through a prismatic lens, but with all the violent and brilliant tones softened. This causes him to view her farther in the distance than she really is, making her appear to him, and to his reader as he paints his vision, as a Marchioness of the eighteenth century.[3]

"Suspiros" (Sighs) expresses the poetic aesthetics of Silva as he explains the techniques he would like to use to write a poem about sighs, a seemingly impossible undertaking. The short composition is very poetic, to the point that it could be called a poem in prose, and it has many ideas which appear in Silva's poems, even, at times, the same turn of phrase. He describes all the different types of sighs of human beings and depicts the

emotions involved. He uses the technique of repetition of lines
and phrases, once repeating nearly a whole paragraph. This
composition expresses an idea often espoused by Silva, that his
poems never satisfied him; they were never as perfect as he
wanted them to be. He believed that it was impossible to express
what he most desired, the ineffable.[4]

In these three compositions of poetic prose, Silva uses the
technique of artistic transpositions, which were such favorites
of the Modernists. Silva shows his Modernist talent in the art
of descriptions, in different tones and shades of colors, using
words as the artist uses a palette of different paints.

There is one other composition by Silva which is somewhat
difficult to classify. The style of writing is not quite as poetic,
and it could perhaps best be classified as an "artículo de costumbres" (sketch about customs). It is entitled "El Paraguas del
Padre León" (The Umbrella of Father León). When Silva was
asked to write for an album that was being prepared to dedicate
to Father León Caiecedo, according to Emilio Cuervo Márquez,
he wrote of the priest, a well-known father of the city of Santa
Fe de Bogotá, and imagined an encounter of the priest with a
modern and luxurious carriage. As it passes Father León, a rich
magnate and his neurasthenic wife look out at him from the
windows. Cuervo Márquez said that a certain Minister felt
himself alluded to, and stopped speaking to Silva. Many people
had informed the Minister about the article, which seemed to
portray him and his wife. For that reason Silva stated that the
only way to write in Bogotá was to write about Spain or some
other country, since if you looked around you and wrote of what
you saw, there was no way to keep someone from feeling that
he or she was being caricatured.[5]

This sketch of the meeting of the priest and the rich carriage
is the closest Silva came to writing an "artículo de costumbres."
First he describes pictorially the priest's appearance in the street,
at the bullfights, and other places, then in his role as father,
officiating at Mass. But Silva judges that when many years have
passed, the only thing which will cause the priest to be remembered will be the memory of him walking under his huge scarlet
umbrella carrying a little green lantern on a gray and rainy
evening in Bogotá, an eighteenth-century apparition. He contrasts

the priest's appearance with the luxurious carriage mentioned above, and uses the contrast to characterize the differences between the eighteenth and nineteenth centuries, symbolizing the transition Bogotá was undergoing in those years.[6]

There is another sketch (or perhaps, stretching the definition somewhat, a short story) entitled "Pataguya" found in the Sunday supplement of *El Espectador,* newspaper of Bogotá. Unfortunately some doubt exists as to whether or not Silva is the author, although the editorial staff of the newspaper testify that the short story was written by Silva.[7] Until disproved, the composition can be accepted as coming from Silva's pen. The plot of the story follows:

In Paris an anonymous narrator who earns his living as a writer relates an encounter with an old school friend whom he does not remember, and who intrudes, interrupting the narrator from the perusal of a book. First, the intruder wants the narrator-author to guess his identity. When he sees that he will never be recognized without help, he tells the narrator that he is Hipólito Mouchat, who studied with him. When the narrator still looks blank, he tells him his nickname, Pataguya, which was the only way the narrator would ever have remembered him. The narrator recalls that Pataguya was the one everyone made fun of, the whipping boy who served as the diversion of the whole school. The only thing the narrator remembered feeling for him was pity.

Beginning to speak to him familiarly, Pataguya causes the author to think of all the miserable experiences of the students in those days, so different from his present, fairly good situation, living in a neighborhood on the Right Bank near the Odeon in Paris. Pataguya continues to remember, with good humor, those persons from their school days. However, in the narrator's mind, they had never even been civil to Pataguya, and had played all kinds of tricks on him. The narrator cannot understand Pataguya's good humor and fond memories. Upon asking where Pataguya lives and what he does for a living, he learns that Pataguya's Right Bank neighborhood is better than his, and Pataguya is employed in a good position. Pataguya intends to marry next year, not a rich girl, but a poor girl who is very good and loves him deeply. She has a paralytic mother and a deaf-and-dumb sister. They are all going to live together so that it will be more economical.

Pataguya cannot understand why the narrator does not have fond memories of the school or of the students and tries to get him to think of one of the most pleasurable things that he experienced in the school. The narrator remembers nothing, and finally Pataguya hints about it being something to eat, but to the narrator none of the food has been very good. A bus stops and the good-hearted clown Pataguya takes a pratfall as he is running for the bus. He is helped up by the driver and a soldier and is still clinging to his cane waving goodbye when the narrator realizes that he did not even offer Pataguya a drink.[8]

There is a double psychological study of the two, the narrator and the obnoxious but good-hearted Pataguya, who forgets all the bad things and only remembers the good. On the contrary, the narrator, in an equally good position in life, is a pessimist and concentrates on the bad things. At first irritated by Pataguya, the narrator finally comes to feel a kind of admiration for Pataguya in his generosity, optimism, and lack of vindictiveness.

Assuming that this short story is by Silva, it is somewhat similar to those stories he translated from Anatole France, with their irony and surprising outcome. At the end of the narration the reader feels sorry for the narrator in his pessimism rather than for Pataguya. The story is quite different from the type of writing Silva did in *De Sobremesa*, but the subject was completely different. Silva did not often write dialogue, and this story is mainly dialogue with the speeches of the two characters reflecting their reactions. The psychological analysis is in the mind of the narrator as well as in the reactions which reflect the psychological mind-set of both characters.

The sophistication and finesse of this analysis are not usually perceived in Silva's works in prose, except for *De Sobremesa*, and there it is solely through the introspective diary of the narrator, and not through the interaction of the narrator in conversation with the persons around him. The charm of the narration does not lie in what is said as much as in what is not said, and has more similarities to the short stories of Anatole France, of Leconte de Lisle, and other ironical French writers than to the prose compositions of Silva

II *Essays on Writers, Introductions to Literary Works and Authors*

Considering the brevity of the pieces Silva wrote about writers, they can only be called sketches rather than critiques, or perhaps notes, since they are so short. But in each, although unscientific in approach, he succeeds in characterizing the writers in an original way, economically and concisely. As any writer does, Silva in these prose essays was contemplating his own feelings and sentiments concerning the subject, coloring them with his stylistic asethetics. But normally a writer does not look only at what he writes, but at his public as well. Silva's ideal public would have been a highly intellectual group of initiates into the sacred Art of literature. But he did not believe that such a public existed in Bogotá, or in Caracas, if we give credence to some of his letters to Sanín Cano. His public was a small group of persons of a high level of literary erudition who shared his artistic sensibilities.

It has been said that every good poet is a critic, and Silva was a profound judge of the literatures of his times. Yet in his sketches and introductions much of his criticism lacked depth, and he did not take these critiques very seriously, perhaps because he did not believe many persons would ever read what he wrote.

Silva was trying in his critical essays to combat vulgarity, lack of comprehension, and lack of respect for the creative art of the writer. These compositions do not have a profound seriousness in tone; however, in several of them there is a broad literary knowledge reflected in Silva's reference to various figures of different literatures. Silva had an exceptional memory, but he did consult libraries; for example, on writing on Rafael Núñez, he spent several days in the library. His sketches or essays are short, usually written for a particular occasion, and his themes are treated in a minor key and without taking himself very seriously.

In "El Doctor Rafael Núñez" we see Núñez as a patriarch, incapable of feeling any emotions not worthy of a retired hero. Silva depicts him as showing little interest in the themes of everyday life, or even in speaking of those men who had been his detractors. But in his discussion with Silva about the glorious

leaders of the past, the material progress of the country, and
the poets and intellectuals, he became animated and seemed to
be twenty years old, rather than his actual sixty-nine. Silva chooses
to leave the political biographers the task of discovering whether or not Núñez felt he had fulfilled all his secret ambitions.
Silva says that the sentiment he observed most clearly in the
titular president the last time he saw him, shortly before his
death, was similar to the poem "Moisés" (Moses): written by
Núñez pointing out his resignation concerning death:

> His heart did not have to suffer;
> Ingratitude more callous than torture
> The laurel, more piercing than the hair shirt
> Could not interrupt his sleep.[9]

In this essay the introductory paragraph is highly compli-
mentary of this many-talented man who became president, a
writer both of poetry and prose. Yet Silva points out that it is
difficult to judge one's contemporaries since the perspective given
by time is absent. Concerning Núñez's poetic works, Silva comments on his lack of soothing music or of correctness of form in
his poems. Ideas at times are difficult to perceive clearly; but
Silva kindly assumes that in this way they are more suggestive.
Silva characterizes the music he displays in his poetry as
that of an organ, and his themes are those of human
passion sublimated by pain. In Núñez's early poems moral problems preoccupied him. Silva describes him in that early period
as tortured by doubt while searching for belief, belief which he
found anew, finally coming to rest again in his Catholic faith.

Silva describes the "quinta" (country house) where the poet-
president lived during the final days before his death in
Cartagena. Silva finds the setting to be ideal in its beauty for the
retired philosopher and poet who has served his country in a
decisive way during the final years of his power.[10]

In "Prólogo *al poema* 'Bienaventurados las que Lloran' " (Prologue to the Poem "Blessed Are They Who Weep") Silva first
characterizes the Sevillan Federico Rivas Frade as being a
popular author for most readers, although admitting that he also
amuses the hard-to-please. Silva mentions that the poet's melancholy is visible in the poems in the volume, as well as his

nostalgic sentiments which often give gladness to the hearts of the readers because of the perfection of his expression of intimate sorrows and feelings all humans have had.

Silva compares Rivas with the Becquerian writers: Heinrich Heine, José Angel Porras, and Antonio Escobar; these are melancholy, suffering poets whom the critics have often compared. Silva feels that not so much active influence is present, but that their similarity of temperament results in the same states of spirit, which cause them to write poems with the same characteristics. They are all "delicate and complicated spirits whose morbid delicacy puts to flight the brutal realities of life."[11]

Silva discusses the impossibility of their finding satisfaction in love, or in nature. Because of the resulting frustrations, they write poems demonstrating their infinite pain and suffering. Their poems are usually short, of one stanza mainly, because according to Silva they have not the patience or energy to write long ones, especially since they are convinced that all human effort is useless.

In Heine, Silva observes that he disguises with irony and violent humor the same interior suffering displayed in the poems of the somewhat more gentle Becquerian writers. Silva attests that these authors are popular with the public and that the poem by Rivas Frade will be appreciated equally well by his readers.

And if the critics within a few weeks begin to discuss Rivas Frade's faults and try to discover whom he imitated, Silva says he will repeat for them one of his poems which has been so popular that many will have learned it. It is a poem in which two persons, once in love, have lost their passionate feelings:

> Looking at our mutual indifference
> It seems to me you think, just as I
> That this world is a masquerade ball
> Or that in both of us our hearts have died.[12]

"Pierre Loti" is a handwritten note found in one of Silva's books and published after his death. Silva begins by pointing out that the enchantment of the novels of Loti is due to the exotic, and, therefore, several of his books will not be long-lived. They are simple studies of ambience without profundity.

His characters, according to Silva, are rudimentary and without strong emotions, serving solely as signs. His "magic" style paints faraway scenes and miniatures. However, Silva feels Loti is not a novelist, because the writer himself is the only character who is clearly visible in his novels, and the one technique redeeming him as a writer is his style of enormous, sensorial feeling, He indicates that perhaps some success might come to Loti because his style is so different from the brutality of the Naturalists. But his novels are also popular for their exotic nature, since Silva is persuaded that anyone would prefer to read of Tahiti than to read a psychological novel with its depiction of surroundings, states of spirit, and endless analysis.[13] Here we observe an ironic critical judgment of the reading public by Silva, who actually felt the opposite, that the most worthwhile works were those which forced the reader to think and take an active part in the work. This the usual reader does not like to do, as Silva reiterated ironically in various works.

The critical essay "Noticia Bibliografica y Literaria [sobre Anatole France]" (Bibliographical and Literary Information [about Anatole France]) serves as an introduction to the short stories which Silva translated from the French of Anatole France, one of his favorite authors. In it Silva names the books written by him, and characterizes them, praising them highly. His novels and short stories have very simple plots and poetic ideas and style. France is ironic in his apt observations of the weaknesses and errors of human beings. The books, according to Silva, correspond to France's definition of the word "books" taken from Littré: "a work of magic from which exude all sorts of images which perturb the spirit and change the heart, or create a magic carpet to take one to the past or to supernatural surroundings."[14]

Silva praises *Thaïs* highly, as his best novel, and perhaps one of the most beautiful which has been written, creating a world within it more real than reality. He comments upon France's severity in criticism of Zola's Naturalism, and reflects upon France's love of beauty and his scorn for strict formulas in art.

Silva is satisfied that France uses any kind of style which pleases him and is thus accused of being a dilettante by the critics. He is censured as a critic of little value because he considers the works of art from so many different points of view, while treating the writers indulgently though ironically. His idiosyncracies of criticism exasperate his adversaries and enemies, but Silva judges that France is in the intellectual vanguard of humanity, similar to the case of Renan. Yet France does not engage in an anguished deliberation of moral problems. He is serenely optimistic, and a good-humored skeptic. Silva questions what these characteristics can be attributed to; the equilibrium of his mental faculties, his temperament, or his life. But Silva does not find an answer to explain why for some writers the same ideas become anguish and torture, and for others the contrary is true. Yet he finds that in France there is a vague melancholy and a sad resignation visible to those who know his works well.[15]

Often there are many similarities between the characterization of Anatole France and the manner in which Silva himself focuses on the writer in his critical essays. They can be accused of dilettantism. A lack of belief in a reading public who would understand what they were saying can also be observed in them.

"El Conde Leon Tolstoi" (Count Leo Tolstoy) is a succinct biography of Tolstoy and a brief account of the historical currents of his time. He considers that two works, *War and Peace* and *Anna Karenina,* mark the supreme moment of the psychic development of the author and the process of evolution which widen his perspective. Both works are summarized, and Silva synthesizes the preoccupations of Tolstoy which are present here as well as in his later works and in the works of those authors who followed him.

Silva reflects upon the social gamut which appears in *War and Peace* and considers it to be an immense panorama of the Russia of the past. *Anna Karenina* is more artistic and, on a smaller scale, depicts the Russian society of twenty years past. Some of his characters in both works are representative of the author with all his doubts and his anguished search for a final answer.

But Tolstoy at one point in his life began to be influenced by certain persons who seemed to have a kind of magic hold on him, and he adopted a new religion of extreme evangelism and of an absurd altruism, a destructive kind of communism which scorned human progress. He became a furious iconoclast. Then he discontinued his artistic work and began to write propagandist pieces against smoking, drinking, and making love. He began to work in the wheat fields and as a shoemaker for children. This singular change, according to Silva, was brought about by his hatred of evil. This hatred of evil caused his intelligence to cede to sentiment and to destroy his creative powers by his own wish. Silva ends the essay with a poetic description of the venerable old man preaching his new religion to the peasants.[16]

The only other essay which approaches literary criticism is a letter to the editor of *El Telegrama* of Medellín. In this letter, Silva disavows having written, and attests that he does not deserve the congratulations sent to him for, a critical article which was published in *La Miscelánea* of Medellín, signed José Luis Ríos. Silva says he never has written criticism and would not publish at any rate in Medellín, but in Bogotá. And he asserts that he would have given his own name if he had written it. He explains his belief that if a pseudonym is used it ought to be solely in the case of a very delicate situation, to avoid hurting someone.

He returns to the question of why he never has written literary crticism. For him, serious criticism is a chore for philosophers, like Taine. The other type of criticism which concerns itself with details and looks for defects seems to him to be a game. One kind of critic in a minor key looks for the funny side of the works he is discussing. Silva then considers several modern French writers one by one, finding the humorous side of each of the poets analyzed. He concludes that criticism is worth very little, and he would exchange two volumes of criticism for one unedited stanza by Bécquer. Silva shows his great erudition concerning the French writers and puts his finger on the humorous defects of several of them.[17] It somehow seems reminiscent of some of Huysmans's much more sarcastic characterizations of French writers.

In "Carta Abierta" (Open Letter), written to Rosa Ponce de Portocarrero,[18] Silva expresses clearly his disinterest in, even dislike for, commercial and political realities, even though he had to think of such things often during and after his bankruptcy. And, on the contrary, he discloses his great love of artistic pursuits to the painter Doña Rosa.

He says to the Señora: "It's that you and I, happier than the others who put their hopes on the unfinished railroad and on the incapable Minister, on the unfruitful sowing season, on the paper money which loses its value, on all those things which interest practical spirits, have the golden key which opens the door of a world that many do not suspect and that others reject."[19]

Clearly, Silva is reflecting his dislike of the commercial world which he was forced to enter by circumstances, and is expressing his feeling that art provides the ideal world. In the following passage that idea is even more clearly expressed: "Now you see how two years later we adore with more fervor what we loved then, and they have lost their illusions."[20]

Silva chides the Señora for having succumbed sometimes to the temptations of riches, and adds that he himself has had "those days in which despairing of ever attaining the harmony of a sentence or the music of a stanza, and having forgotten my poets, I have sinned gravely, and I have lost my ardor, without strength to resist the giddy temptations of Gold."[21]

But Silva says he has reestablished his interior peace through counseling from his lay confessor, and by reading and meditating upon these lines from the *Imitation of Christ*: "Spiritual consolations exceed all the delights of the world and the sensuality of the flesh. Not all the delights of the world are vain or base."[22]

In this short selection, as in others of his prose compositions, Silva demonstrates his high level of literary culture, as can be observed by his citation of Thomas à Kempis in Latin, his delicate expression, and above all his attitude of spirit which shows that he is on guard against vulgarity and is consoling himself against vicissitudes of life in his moral meditations.

This letter is different from some of Silva's literary letters in that it is an apology for art as opposed to more mundane affairs. In a way it is not actually a letter but a literary disquisition written for a particular occasion, and on that basis communicates a message to his readers as well as to a person who apparently felt the same way he did about art.

Silva translated five of Anatole France's short stories, two from *El Cofre de Nacar* (The Mother-of-Pearl Box): "La Misa de las Sombras" (The Mass of the Ghosts) and "El Saltimbanqui de Nuestra Señora" (Our Lady's Clown); three from *Balthasar*: "La Reseda del Cura" (The Priest's Mignonette), and two whose titles are proper names: "Loeta Acilia" and "Balthasar."[23] In these translations, upon comparing the two languages, French and Spanish, Silva reflects the excellence of his knowledge of French. Usually the translations are literal, but with an outstanding choice of poetic vocabulary. However, he occasionally adds clarifying phrases which often would not really be necessary if he were trying to translate literally. He was so much of a stylist that he added beauty of color and sound where he could, even at the expense of fidelity to the text. In his translation of "La Misa de las Sombras" there appears an example of his usage of words to add clarity:

La muerte no los asusta, por-   (Death does not frighten them be-
que a fuerza de verla de cerca   cause by dint of seeing it closely
y a cada rato, no se acuerdan   so often, they never remember it.)
nunca de ella.[24]

In the French the sentence is more concise, less amplified:

La mort ne les effraye point;   (Death does not frighten them at
ils n'y pensent jamais.[25]   all; they never think of it.)

In the example from "Balthasar" which follows, Silva added color and sound in his translation, making the passage more aesthetically pleasing to himself and to his readers:

Venìa a la cabeza Abner, que   (Abner was leading the group; he
se prosternó tres veces a los   bowed humbly three times at the
pies de Balkis e hizo que le   feet of Balkis and had them bring
acercaran un palanquín cubier-   over a litter covered with purple
to de púrpura y de paño de oro   and golden cloth which they brought
que traían listo para llevarla.[26]   with them, ready to bear her away.)

The Frence sentence is much more concise and lacks the vocabulary reflecting color and sound:

Il se prosterna trois fois aux   (He bowed humbly three times at
pieds de Balkis et fit avancer   the feet of Balkis and had them
prés d'elle una litière pré-   bring near to her a litter prepared
parée pour la recevoir.[27]   to receive her.)

Silva did not actually perform treason, as the saying goes, in his translations, for by his use of more descriptive words and phrases he improved the text, writing at times his own version of what was taking place in the stories he translated. Daniel Arias Argáez says that Silva translated from the short stories of Paul Margueritte as well, but none of these has been found.[28] A short story by Silva mentioned earlier, entitled "Pataguya," was found,[29] but without adequate documentation to prove definitely that the work was not, rather, translated by Silva. Among the collections of short stories by Paul Margueritte which were examined by this author, none is to be found which matches the text of "Pataguya," but some are similar in tone or type to this short sketch. Yet in the absence of proof to the contrary, this short story must be accepted as one of Silva's original stories or versions, although it is quite different from anything else which he is known to have written.

In conclusion, in this miscellany of prose, Silva writes at least two different types of prose. In one he writes with more emotion, as for example in his compositions in which he defends ideas of deep feeling: the sacredness of art and the profanation of the Muse by irony. In another, he is the pure intellectual. One example of this is his letter to the newspaper, denying his authorship of an article, and at the same time including a brief, humorous critique of several of the French poets of the epoch. These two types of prose reflect two sides of his personality. First, there is the translator, investigator, avid reader, and student of literature who is also a critic of minor tone. Second, there is the creator and artist, and it seems that this is his dominant, or perhaps just more successful, side.

CHAPTER 6

Summation

I T is often difficult to counteract the overemphasis on the life of Silva and its vicissitudes. Also present are the legends created about him, which in turn detract attention from his work. Yet he was a major Modernist writer, and one of those whose poetry has stood the test of time, perhaps because much of it is contemporary in theme and content. The impetus for twentieth-century poetic innovations came from the Modernists, and among them Silva can be judged as one who considerably affected the poetry of following generations, although his influence was admittedly slight during most of his lifetime, arousing interest in literary circles only during the four or five years preceding his death.

The significance of his work could not be appreciated until after his death because he had published comparatively little during his lifetime. But after the first publication of his *Poesías* (Poems), in Spain in 1908,[1] he began to be considered seriously as a major Modernist writer. That first edition awakened interest in Spain and Spanish America. The prologue was by Miguel de Unamuno,[2] but the editors had collected only forty-five of his poems and had made various changes in the texts. For that reason, the Spanish critic's judgment was not validly based on a completely representative selection of his poems. Many of those who had the opportunity to read the edition depended on the partial view in the prologue by Unamuno, who said that he was unaware of what Modernism meant, but that he found some of the same things in Silva as in the writers called Modernists. He pointed out that while he disliked them in the others, he liked them in Silva.

Later, in the 1940s, Juan Ramón Jiménez[3] and others began to exalt the value of the works of Silva, especially the "Nocturno"

154

(Nocturne). Jiménez, as well as other critics, felt that Silva had added a new dimension to heroic poetry in his poem dedicated to Bolívar, because celebrating Bolívar's failures thereby added a new human dimension to the hero. After these critics began to perceive Silva's stature, he became one of the most discussed Modernists by Spanish-American critics as well as those of many other nationalities.

It is true that much of Silva's fame rests on one poem, perhaps the best poem in the Spanish language, although as observed in the analysis of his other poems, many display the same extraordinary talent. He might have called these poems his jewels, as he spoke of some of those which sank with the ship *L'Amerique.* In this one masterwork and in others of his best poems, Silva expresses in a creative manner an intense vision of significant themes and conflicts of human beings. There is considerable variety in his themes, as has been noted, from the paradise lost of childhood to his meditations on the mysteries of life. Also to be observed is his pessimism due to the brevity of life and the fleetingness of affections, joined with the certainty of death. He demonstrates his disappointment and disillusionment with various aspects of life.

In some of his poems, "Gotas Amargas" (Bitter Potions) and in a few other poems of ironic tone, the poet confronts the reader with his intimate rejection of the social order and a disillusionment with the comportment of persons within that social order. It is easy to observe a long poetic descent from these bitter poems. In Colombia, there was Luis Carlos López, and in other countries there were poets following his lead, at least in some of their poems. These included, among others, Salvador Díaz Mirón of Mexico, Carlos Pezoa Vélez, and in the present, Nicanor Parra, the latter two writers from Chile.

De Sobremesa (After-Dinner Chat) and Silva's other prose was typically Modernist in style and content but, aside from the novel, his prose compositions were brief and his production was not voluminous. His short essays reflect a mature Modernist expression because of their sculptured qualities, their coloristic techniques, and the self-consciousness of these and other individualistic traits. *De Sobremesa* was not published until 1925,[4] when Modernism was waning. It had been reconstructed the

year before Silva's death, after having been lost when the
L'Amerique sank. It has been thought that it is a mélange which
Silva put together from memory out of a number of different
manuscripts, including the manuscript of *De Sobremesa*. It is
admittedly not an outstanding Modernist novel, and is perhaps
read and studied only because it is by Silva. Yet it reflects many
of the characteristics of the typical end-of-century hero; the volup-
tuosity, intellectualism, and yearning for life. The work offers
a surprising contrast between the self-consciously ornate and
aesthetic prose writer, and the poet who writes a deceptively
simple, natural, yet Symbolist kind of poetry.

One must consider his poetry primarily in assessing his influence on succeeding generations of Spanish American writers.
Similarities can be seen in each of the poets who express a comparable intensity in their meditations on life and death and
the problems of the individual human being. And in several of
these poets, such preoccupations are joined, just as in Silva and
the other Modernists, with a profound desire to present those
ideas in the most appropriate form, and to unite completely form,
rhythm, and content. This stress of the Modernists on that type
of unity is reflected in the works of many later Spanish and
Spanish-American poets. The Modernists' preoccupation with
style and their desire for extreme individuality and originality can
also be said to have stimulated analogous concerns in succeeding
generations of poets.

Notes and References

Chapter One

1. Federico de Onís, "Introducción," in *Antología de la Poesía Española e Hispanoamericana (1882–1932)* (New York, 1961), p. xviii.
2. Rubén Darío, *Prosas Profanas y Otros Poemas* (Buenos Aires, 1896).
3. José Asunción Silva, *De Sobremesa, 1887–1896 (After-Dinner Chat)* (1st ed., Bogotá, 1925; 2nd ed., Bogotá, [1928]).
4. Manuel Díaz Rodríquez, *Idolos Rotos* (2nd ed., Madrid, 1919. The first edition, now out of print, was published in 1901).

Chapter Two

1. In Book 14, page 11 of the Baptism Book of the Iglesia de Nuestra Señora de las Nieves (Church of Our Lady of the Snows) is the following entry:

In the home of Ricardo Silva, on January 6, 1866, the Presbyter Trino de la C. Martínez, licensed by the Illustrious Archbishop, solemnly baptized a boy of forty-one days, legitimate son of Ricardo Silva and Vicenta Gómez Diago, and they named him: José Asunción Salustiano Facundo. Paternal grandparents: [José] Asunción Silva Fortoul and María de Jesús Frade; maternal: Vicente Antonio Gómez Restrepo and Mercedes Diago. Godparents were: Salustiano Villar de la Torre and Mercedes Diago de Gómez. They were advised of their responsibilities. I bear witness. Fernando Ignacio Castañeda.

Since the child was forty-one days old on January 6, his birthdate had to be November 26 and not November 27, as Alberto Miramón attests in his biography of Silva, the most complete and authoritative in existence, entitled: *José Asunción Silva: Ensayo Biográfico con Documentos Inéditos*, 1st ed. (Bogotá, 1937). Subsequent references to this work will use the author's name and the page numbers. Some critics have given without foundation the dates October 26 and 27 for Silva's birth.

2. Miramón, pp. 11–12.
3. Ibid., p. 8.

4. Ibid., pp. 8–10.

5. Ibid., p. 6.

6. The first edition of Ricardo Silva's *Articulos de Costumbres* was published in Bogotá in 1883 by Silvestre and Co., and was dedicated to his son. The latest edition by the same title, also dedicated to his son was published in Bogotá in 1973.

7. Miramón, p. 6.

8. Ibid., p. 3.

9. Ibid., p. 19.

10. Ibid.

11. Baldomero Sanín Cano, "José Asunción Silva," *Revista de las Indias*, Bogotá, Vol. 28, No. 89, p. 162.

12. Ibid.

13. Miramón, p. 65.

14. See the comments made by Silva for his protagonist of *De Sobremesa, 1887–1896*, 2nd ed. (Bogotá, 1925), p. 127, where José Fernández speaks of "an intellectual cultivation sought without method and with the crazy idea of reaching universality."

15. Baldomero Sanín Cano, "José Asunción Silva, en el Cincuentenario de su Muerte," p. 163.

16. Miramón, p. 27.

17. Emilio Cuervo Márquez, "José Asunción Silva: Su Vida y su Obra," in *Ensayos y Conferencias* (Bogotá, 1937), p. 218.

18. Daniel Arias Argáez, "Cincuentenario de la Muerte de José Asunción Silva," *Registro Municipal*, Bogotá, June 30, 1946, p. 247.

19. Miramón, pp. 26–27.

20. José Asunción Silva, *Poesiás Completas Seguidas de Prosas Selectas*, 3rd ed. (Madrid, 1963), p. 141.

21. Baldomero Sanín Cano, "José Asunción Silva," in *De mi Vida y Otras Vidas* (Bogotá, 1949), p. 41.

22. José Asunción Silva, *Poesiás Completas Seguidas de Prosas Selectas*, 3rd ed. (Madrid, 1963), p. 38.

23. Baldomero Sanín Cano, "José Asunción Silva," *Revista de las Indias*, Bogotá, Vol. 28, No. 89, May, 1946, p. 164.

24. Miramón, p. 40.

25. See "Condolencia en la Muerte de Don Antonio María Silva," *Papel Periódico Ilustrado*, Vol. 4, No. 80, Dec. 1, 1884, pp. 127–28.

26. Camilo de Brigard Silva, "El Infortunio Comercial de Silva," Part 1, *La Revista de América*, Bogotá, Vol. 6, No. 17, May, 1946, p. 282.

27. Ibid.

28. Juan Evangelista Manrique, "José Asunción Silva: Recuerdos

Intimos," *La Revista de América*, Paris, Vol. 6, January, 1914, pp. 32–37.

29. Camilo de Brigard Silva, "El Infortunio Comercial de Silva," Part 1, *La Revista de América*, Bogotá, Vol. 6, No. 17, May 1946, pp. 282–83.

30. Ibid., p. 283.

31. Miramón, pp. 65–66.

32. Tomás Rueda Vargas in "El Silva que yo Conocí," en *Pasando el Rato* (Bogotá, 1925), says on p. 98: "Many times we have heard him called affected, effeminate by women, and within the epoch these epithets fit him exactly and were just."

33. Daniel Arias Argáez, "Cincuentenario de la Muerte de José Asunción Silva," *Registro Municipal*, Bogotá, June 30, 1946, p. 252.

34. Baldomero Sanín Cano, "Recuerdos de José Asunción Silva," *Manizales*, Manizales, Colombia, December, 1945, p. 80.

35. See a reproduction of this drawing which accompanies one of his short prose compositions entitled: "Carta Abierta," contributed by Germán Arciniegas to *Universidad*, Bogotá, No. 104, October 20, 1928, pp. 486–88.

36. All three translations or versions were published in *Papel Periódico Ilustrado*, Bogotá: December 16, 1882, a version of "Las Golondrinas," by Pierre Jean Béranger. On August 20, 1883, the poet published "Imitación," a version of a poem by Maurice de Guérin. On July 24, 1885, a version of "Realidad" by Victor Hugo appeared. These versions, and Silva's ability as a translator, will be discussed in Chapter Three.

37. José María Rivas Groot, ed., *La Lira Nueva* (Bogotá, 1886), pp. 373–92.

38. Baldomero Sanín Cano, "José Asunción Silva," in *De mi Vida y Otras Vidas* (Bogotá, 1949), p. 41.

39. See "La Protesta de la Musa," *Revista Literaria*, Bogotá, Vol. 2, December 14, 1890, pp. 133–35.

40. Daniel Arias Argáez, "Cincuentenario de la Muerte de José Asunción Silva," p. 257.

41. Although in the "Chronology" of Miramón's book, pp. 189–90, the date of Ricardo Silva's death is given as 1889, in the text it is 1887, and the author stated in a personal interview that the date in the "Chronology" was a typographical error. Further investigation reevaled the truth of his statement. However, many students of the work of Silva continue to use the 1889 date since it has been cited erroneously from Miramón's "Chronology" many times.

42. Miramón, p. 190.

43. Camilo de Brigard Silva, "El Infortunio Comercial de Silva," Part 2, *La Revista de América*, Vol. 6, No. 18, June 1946, p. 298.

44. Although this publication has been cited many times, it was found only recently. Hector H. Orjuela was given the information concerning its location by the Colombian Miguel Arbeláez Sarmiento. This led to its being discovered by Professor Orjuela. The "Nocturno" appears in *Lectura para Todos*, Cartagena, Colombia, Year 2, No. 7, pp. 50–51.

45. See the six unnumbered photocopied pages of the manuscript in Isaacs's handwriting following page 362 in José Asunción Silva, *Obras Completas* (Bogotá, 1965). The typewritten text of the poem of 131 lines is given complete in Miramón, pp. 98–101.

46. Daniel Arias Argáez, "Cincuentenario de la Muerte de José Asunción Silva," p. 249.

47. Miramón, pp. 120–21.

48. Camilo de Brigard Silva, "El Infortunio Comercial de Silva," Part 2, *La Revista de América*, Bogotá, Vol. 6, No. 18, June 1946, p. 298.

49. Rufino Blanco Fombona, *El Modernismo y los Poetas Modernistas* (Madrid, 1929), pp. 115–16.

50. José Asunción Silva, *Poesías*, Precedidas de un Prólogo por Miguel de Unamuno (Barcelona, 1908).

51. Emilio Cuervo Márquez, *Ensayos y Conferencias*, p. 214. One year earlier, Alvaro Holguín y Caro in "La Muerte de José Asunción Silva," *Revista del Colegio Mayor de Nuestra Señora del Rosario*, Vol. 31, Nos. 306, 307, August 1936, p. 392, affirmed that the legend of incest originated in the mind of the Venezuelan critic Rufino Blanco Fombona.

52. Alejandro C. Arias, "José Asunción Silva," in *Ensayos: Goethe, José Asunción Silva, Stefan Zweig* (Salto, Uruguay, 1936), pp. 89–110.

53. Max Daireaux, *Littérature Hispano-Américaine* (Paris, 1930), pp. 92–93.

54. Ricardo Gullón, *Direcciones del Modernismo* (Madrid, 1963), p. 87.

55. Daniel Arias Argáez, "Cincuentenario de la Muerte de José Asunción Silva," p. 265.

56. Miramón, p. 96.

57. Ibid., p. 95.

58. Ibid., p. 96.

59. Ibid., p. 105.

60. Daniel Arias Argáez, "Cincuentenario de la Muerte de José Asunción Silva," p. 262.

61. Carlos García Prada, "Introducción," in José Asunción Silva, *Prosas y Versos* (Mexico City, 1942), p. xxi.

62. Daniel Arias Argáez, "Cincuentenario de la Muerte de José Asunción Silva," p. 262.

63. Miramón, pp. 87–89.

64. Ibid., p. 103.

65. Camilo de Brigard Silva, "El Infortunio Comercial de Silva," Part 1, *La Revista de América*, Bogotá, Vol. 6, No. 17, May 1946, pp. 281–88; Part 2, *La Revista de América*, Bogotá, Vol. 6, No. 18, June 1946, pp. 289–300.

66. Camilo de Brigard Silva, "El Infortunio Comercial de Silva," Part 2, p. 296.

67. Ibid., pp. 290–94.

68. José Asunción Silva, *Obras Completas,* Banco de la República, pp. 369–70. In a letter to his mother, after having taken the diplomatic post in Caracas, Silva talks of going to visit Rafael Núñez and of showing him some of the rare books he had brought back with him from Europe, books which no one else in Colombia owned.

69. Emilio Cuervo Márquez, *Ensayos y Conferencias*, p. 218.

70. Miramón, p. 121.

71. José Asunción Silva, "El Doctor Rafael Núñez," *El Cojo Ilustrado,* Caracas, Vol. 3, No. 67, December 1, 1894, pp. 379–80.

72. "El Cofre de Nacar," in *Biblioteca Popular: Colección de Grandes Escritores,* Vol. 2 (Bogotá, 1893), pp. 1–31.

73. See note 44.

74. Ricardo Riaño Jauma, "José Asunción Silva," *Revista Bimestre Cubana,* Vol. 51, March-April 1943, p. 244.

75. José Asunción Silva, *Obras Completas*, Banco de la República, 1965, p. 375.

76. Miramón, pp. 141–42.

77. Ibid., p. 150.

78. Ibid., p. 152.

79. Ibid., p. 161.

80. See José Asunción Silva, *Poesiás,* Precididas de un Prólogo por Miguel de Unamumo (Barcelona, 1908). The poems published during Silva's lifetime had not all been found in 1908, nor had all those he had written been discovered. The same thing can be said at the present time, but at least fifty-three additional poems have been uncovered through investigation since 1908.

81. See the two editions prepared by Carlos García Prada, *Prosas y Versos* (1st ed., Mexico City, 1942; 2nd ed., Madrid, 1960).

82. See *De Sobremesa, 1887–1896* (1st ed., Bogotá, 1925; 2nd ed., Bogotá [1928]).

83. Baldomero Sanín Cano, "José Asunción Silva," in *De mi Vida y Otras Vidas* (Bogotá, 1949), p. 47.

84. Donald McGrady, "Sobre una Alusión Literaria en la Novela Pax," *Revista Iberoamericana*, Vol. 29, No. 55, January-June 1963, pp. 147–56.

85. Juan Evangelista Manrique, "José Asunción Silva: Recuerdos Intimos," *La Revista de América*, Paris, Vol. 6, January 1914, p. 41.

86. Daniel Arias Argáez, "Cincuentenario de la Muerte de José Asunción Silva," p. 264.

87. Miramón, p. 167.

88. Ibid, p. 155.

89. Ricardo Riaño Jauma, "José Asunción Silva," *Revista Bimestre Cubana*, Vol. 11, March–April 1943, p. 245.

90. Ibid.

91. Guillermo Valencia, "José Asunción Silva," *Nosotros*, Buenos Aires, Vol. 4, Year 3, 1909, p. 166.

92. Miramón, pp. 159–60.

93. Alcides Arguedas, "La Muerte de José Asunción Silva," *Atenea*, Concepción, Chile, Vol. 26, No. 106, April 1934, p. 188.

94. Emilio Cuervo Márquez, *Ensayos y Conferencias*, p. 227.

Chapter Three

1. In the bibliography of this book will be listed those editions which seem to be the most authentic, least mutilated. For a fuller bibliography, in which several of the thirty-six editions listed are annotated, refer to Betty Tyree Osiek, *José Asunción Silva: Estudio Estilístico de su Poesía*, Mexico City: Ediciones de Andrea, 1968, pp. 186–204. It is the most comprehensive listing prepared until the present time, although understandably covering only through 1968. It contains 206 studies on Silva. In further notes concerning bibliographical information, it will be referred to by the author's surname and a shortened title.

2. José Asunción Silva, *Poesiás* (Barcelona, 1908).

3. Hector H. Orjuela, ed., *Poesiás*, Biblioteca "Colombia Literaria" (Bogotá, 1973). Since this is the most complete edition, the majority of the poetry citations will be taken from this work, and will be indicated henceforth solely by the page numbers in the text.

4. Guillermo Valencia in "José Asunción Silva," *Nosotros*, Buenos Aires, Year 3, Vol. 4, 1909, p. 170, condemns the mutilation of the

first edition, and mentions several names of "Gotas Amargas" which were suppressed, some of which have never been found.

5. In October, 1977, an edition of Silva's poetry edited by Hector Orjuela was published which included thirty-three inedited compositions from the notebook containing these adolescent poems attributed to Silva. Because of the late date of publication, the work, entitled *Intimidades,* Serie "La Granada Entreabierta," 18 (Bogotá, 1977) was unavailable for consultation before this book had reached the stage of galley proofs. For that reason, twenty-seven poems and six translations from among the fifty-nine included in *Intimidades* are not discussed in Chapter Three.

6. *El Libro de Versos,* facsimile edition of the manuscript, without pagination (Bogotá, 1945), [68 pp.].

7. This author has examined the original manuscript of *De Sobremesa* at two different times in the home of Camilo de Brigard Silva, now deceased. Also seen and collated with the facsimile edition mentioned in note 5 was the original of the manuscript of *El Libro de Versos,* in the home of a well-known literary figure in a country far from Colombia.

8. See the Chronology for the listing of all these poems and translations which appeared during Silva's lifetime.

9. *Poesías* (Barcelona, [1910]); *Poesías* (Barcelona, [1918]); *Poesías* (Barcelona, [1918?]. See Osiek, *Estudio Estilístico,* p. 186, for descriptive annotations of these three editions.

10. *Poesías,* Definitive edition, Prologue by Miguel de Unamuno, and Notes by Baldomero Sanín Cano (Paris, 1923). The later editions based on this one include: *Poesías,* Definitive edition, Study by Baldomero Sanín Cano (Santiago, Chile, 1923); *Poesías y Prosas* (Montevideo, n.d.); two editions edited by Carlos García Prada, *Prosas y Versos,* 1st ed. (Mexico City, 1942); *Prosas y Versos,* 2nd ed. (Madrid, 1960); *Poesías Completas* (1st ed., Buenos Aires, 1941; 2nd ed., 1943; 3rd ed., 1945; 4th ed., 1950).

11. *El Libro de Versos, 1883–1896* (Bogotá, [1928], 1946); *El Libro de Versos y Otras Poesías* (Madrid, 1954).

12. *Poesías Completas Seguidas de Prosas Selectas,* Madrid, 1st ed., 1951; 2nd ed., 1952; 3rd ed., 1963).

13 Orjuela, ed., *Poesías* (see above note 3).

14. *Obras Completas* (Bogotá, 1965).

15. Donald McGrady, " 'Crepúsculo,' Otro Poema Olvidado de José Asunción Silva," *Thesaurus: Boletín del Instituto Caro y Cuervo,* Bogotá, Vol. 29, No. 2, May-August 1974, pp. 350–53. Professor McGrady informs us of the notebooks of poems of Silva's adolescence,

of which there was one in Silva's handwriting, and another in the handwriting of the two friends whom Silva allowed to copy the poems: Paca Martín and María Manrique. These notebooks passed from hand to hand and finally have disappeared. They were said to contain fifteen poems with numbers, under the general title "Notas Perdidas," as well as several others with individual titles. From this notebook five of the numbered "Notas Perdidas" have been published, and nine of those with titles. They have appeared in such Colombian periodicals as *Revista Ilustrada*, 1898, and *Universidad*, 1928. The location of these first publications of the little-known and rarely collected poems among them will be given when the poems are analyzed.

16. Guillermo Valencia, "José Asunción Silva," *Nosotros*, Buenos Aires, Year 3, Vol. 4, 1909, p. 165. Bernardo Gicovate also attests that these poems have no value except as proof of the poems a precocious child and adolescent can write. His opinion appears in *Conceptos Fundamentales de Literatura Comparada: Iniciación de la Poesía Modernista* (San Juan, Puerto Rico, 1962), p. 119.

17. Luis Alberto Sánchez, "La Idea de la Muerte en José Asunción Silva," *Cuadernos Americanos*, Mexico City, Vol. 79, No. 1, Jan.-Feb. 1955, p. 275.

18. Miramón, p. 152.

19. Osiek, *Estudio Estilístico*, pp. 121–36, includes this poem and twelve other unknown and forgotten poems which are definitely by Silva, as well as parts of three others which are somewhat doubtful. All were discovered in different Colombian periodicals, and most of them had not been included in previous collections. One of the poems, which begins "Que por qué no publico versos . . .," was later proved not to have been written by Silva, and "Rien du Tout" had Silva's authorship thrown into serious doubt by Donald McGrady in "Cuatro Notas Acerca de Algunos Poemas Atribuidos a José Asunción Silva," in *Thesaurus: Boletín del Instituto Caro y Cuervo*, Bogotá, Vol. 24, No. 3, Sept.-Dec. 1969, pp. 469–80. The twelve poems and parts of three others were discovered earlier, appearing in Osiek, "A Stylistic Study of Silva's Poetry," Dissertation, Washington University, 1966. However, Professor McGrady and others have been investigating and searching out the scattered poems published by Silva in different Colombian periodicals. McGrady's investigations led to the publication of a series of articles beginning in 1966 (see bibliography), in which he documents the finding of most of those same poems found by Osiek, and another nine poems, some with doubts as to their authorship. Professor Hector Orjuela was another of the investigators who made significant discoveries; among others,

he found the date and the periodical in which appeared for the first time the famous "Nocturno." Credit will be given in chronological order to the discoverers of these forgotten poems (shortening the bibliographical information when possible). "Perdida" was also found by McGrady in "Diez Poesías Olvidadas de José Asunción Silva," *Thesarus: Boletín del Instituto Caro y Cuervo*, Bogotá, Vol. 23, No. 1, Jan.–Apr. 1968, pp. 58–59. The poem also appears in Orjuela, *Poesías*, pp. 141–42. The poem was discovered in *Universidad*, No. 106, Nov. 8, 1928, p. 540.

20. Donald McGrady, "Tres Poemas Atribuidos a José Asunción Silva," *Thesaurus: Boletín del Instituto Caro y Cuervo*, Bogotá, Vol. 27, No. 1, Jan.–Apr. 1972, p. 107. It is included in Orjuela, *Poesías*, pp. 156–57. The poem appeared in *La Musa Americana*, Bogotá, Vol. 4, No. 24, March 1906, p. 2.

21. Osiek, *Estudio Estilístico*, p. 123; Orjuela, in *Poesías*, also gives the final three stanzas in a note on p. 125.

22. Osiek, *Estudio Estilístico*, p. 125; McGrady, "Diez Poesías Olvidadas," p. 60; Orjuela, *Poesías*, p. 146.

23. Osiek, *Estudio Estilístico*, pp. 126–27; McGrady, "Diez Poesías Olvidadas," pp. 61–62; Orjuela, *Poesías*, pp. 147–48.

24. Osiek, *Estudio Estilístico*, pp. 125–26; McGrady, "Diez Poesías Olvidadas," pp. 60–61; Orjuela, *Poesías*, pp. 146–47.

25. Luis Alberto Sánchez proposed in "La Idea de la Muerte en José Asunción Silva," *Cuadernos Americanos*, Mexico City, Vol 79, No. 1, Jan.–Feb., 1955, pp. 278–80, that Silva might have had syphilis himself. Sánchez believed that venereal diseases were referred to in several of the "Gotas Amargas." But it seems to this author that the critic is setting up another legend which has no proof, although his aim seems to be to destroy in this manner the legends of Silva's misogyny and his incestuous passion for his sister Elvira.

26. Horacio Botero Isaza, *José Asunción Silva* (Medellín, 1919), p. 22.

27. Carlos E. Restrepo, "Reminiscencias sobre Jose Asunción Silva," *Repertorio Americano*, Vol. 1, San José, Costa Rica, Vol. 1, No. 2, Sept. 11, 1919, pp. 24–25.

28. François Coppée, "La Réponse de la Terre," *Oeuvres*, Vol. 3, *Poesías, 1874–1878* (Paris, n.d.), pp. 24–25.

29. See the hypothesis of McGrady in "Cuatro Notas Acerca de Algunos Poemas Atribuidos a José Asunción Silva," *Thesaurus: Boletín del Instituto Caro y Cuervo*, Bogotá, Vol. 24, No. 3, Sept.–Dec. 1969, pp. 468–69.

30. This poem was discovered by McGrady in *Gil Blas*, Vol. 3,

No. 247, May 24, 1912, and was discussed by him in "Two Unknown Poems by José Asunción Silva," *Modern Language Notes*, Vol. 81, No. 2, March 1966. He testifies that the poems published in *Gil Blas* are: "Paseo," "El Recluta," "Avant-Propos," "Egalité," "Resurrexit," "Idilio," "Madrigal," "Necedad Yanqui," "Psicoterapéutica," and "Zoospermos." In that article McGrady states that of these poems, only "El Recluta" and "Avant-Propos" had been published previously. However, "Idilio," called by one editor "Vida Aldeana," to distinguish it from the "Idilio" which is one of the "Gotas Amargas," was actually published in *Revista Ilustrada*, Bogotá, Year 1, Vol. 1, June 18, 1898, as Professor McGrady later discovered and attested in "Diez Poesías Olvidadas de José Asunción Silva," pp. 51–52. The other poems he mentions, except for "Paseo," were published for the first time in book form in the 1918 edition by Maucci, under the heading "Gotas Amargas," and probably some were taken from *Gil Blas* as well as other periodicals. However, in that edition two of those were not included, perhaps because of some doubt that they are by Silva or because they were not from among the best of Silva's production. These poems are: "Resurrexit" and "Necedad Yanqui."

31. McGrady, "Tres Poemas Atribuidos a José Asunción Silva," *Thesaurus: Boletín del Instituto Caro y Cuervo*, Bogotá, Vol. 27, No. 1, Jan.–Apr. 1972, pp. 104–108. According to McGrady, and also discovered there by this author, the facsimile of the poem in Silva's handwriting was included in *Pan*, Bogotá, No. 23, August 1938, p. 115.

32. Guillermo Valencia, "José Asunción Silva," *Nosotros*, Buenos Aires, Year 3, Vol. 4, 1909, p. 174.

33. Arturo Torres Rioseco has pointed out what he believes to be a parallelism between Silva and Poe through the vehicle of the translations of Poe's poetry by Mallarmé and Baudelaire, in "La Teorías Poéticas de Poe y el Caso de José Asunción Silva," *Ensayos sobre Literatura Latinamericana* (Mexico City, 1953), pp. 65–74. He believes that Silva found in them an exceptional guide to enter into the evolution of French Symbolism.

34. McGrady, "Diez Poesiás Olvidadas," pp. 53–56. Orjuela, *Poesías*, pp. 71–72. This poem was published in *Revista Literaria*, Vol. 1, No. 3, 1898, pp. 45–46.

35. Baldomero Sanín Cano, "José Asunción Silva," in *Poesías* (Santiago, Chile, 1923), pp. 11–12.

36. Osiek, *Estudio Estilístico*, p. 129; McGrady, "Diez Poesías Olvidades," pp. 9–10; Orjuela, Poesías, p. 133. This poem appeared in *Universidad*, No. 106, November 8, 1928, p. 538.

37. McGrady, "Diez Poesías Olvidadas," pp. 5–6; Orjuela, *Poesías,* pp. 143–44. Although this is similar to many of Silva's poems from his earlier period in style and tone, there is something about it which lacks the inner melancholy, the veiled pessimism, which often appears in his poems of that early period. But in the absence of definite proof to the contrary, one must accept it as one of Silva's.

38. Homero Castillo, "El Tema de Lázaro en un Poema de José Asunción Silva," *Hispania,* Vol. 50, No. 2, May 1967, pp. 262–65.

39. Horacio Botero Isaza, *José Asunción Silva* (Medellín, 1919), p. 17.

40. Leon Dierx, *Oeuvres Complètes,* Vol. 1, *Poèmes et Poésies, Les Lèvres Closes* (Paris, n.d.), pp. 127–29.

41. This poem first appeared in *Revista Ilustrada,* Bogotá, Year 1, Vol. 1, No. 3, August 1898, p. 46.

42. Osiek, *Estudio Estilístico,* pp. 132–33; McGrady, "Diez Poesías Olvidadas," pp. 4–5. This poem was published in *Revista Ilustrada,* Vol. 1, No. 1, 1898, p. 15, with the title "Idilio," It also appeared in *Revista Chilena,* Santiago, Chile, Vol. 2, No. 7, Oct. 1917, pp. 191–92, with the title "Vida Aldeana," probably given by the editor in order to distinguish it from the poem with the same title which is one of the "Gotas Amargas."

43. Osiek, *Estudio Estilístico,* pp. 128–29; Orjuela, *Poesías,* pp. 138–39. This poem was published in the two articles by Daniel Arias Argáez: "Cincuentenario de la Muerte de José Asunción Silva," *Registro Municipal,* Bogotá, June 30, 1946, pp. 242–65; "Recuerdos de José Asunción Silva," *Bolívar,* Bogotá, Vol. 5, Nov.-Dec. 1951, pp. 939–64. In citing these two articles, where several unknown and forgotten poems were published for the first time, the titles will be shortened after this note to "Cincuentenario" and "Recuerdos."

44. McGrady, "Tres Poemas Atribuidos a José Asunción Silva," *Thesaurus: Boletín del Instituto Caro y Cuervo,* Vol. 27, No. 1, Jan.–Apr. 1972, pp. 105–106; Orjuela, *Poesías,* p. 151. The poem appeared in two Colombian periodicals in the same year: *El Nuevo Tiempo Literario,* Vol. 5, 1907, p. 26, and in *El Correo del Valle,* Cali, Vol. 13, 1907, p. 2921.

45. McGrady, " 'Crepúsculo,' Otro Poema Olvidado de José Asunción Silva," *Thesaurus: Boletín del Instituto Caro y Cuervo,* Vol. 29, No. 2, Bogotá, May–Aug. 1974, pp. 350–53. The poem cited was published in *Lecturas Dominicales, Literary Supplement* of *El Tiempo,* Vol. 3, No. 55, May 25, 1924, pp. 72–73.

46. As Orjuela notes in the Cosmos edition of the *Poesías* of Silva which he edited, p. 148, this poem was found separately by both him

and Miguel Arbeláez Sarmiento in *El Telegrama,* Bogotá, No. 131, Nov. 24, 1886.

47. Osiek, *Estudio Estilístico,* p. 133; Orjuela, *Poesías,* p. 150. This poem appeared in Arias Argáez, "Cincuentenario," p. 249, and "Recuerdos," p. 946.

48. Osiek, *Estudio Estilístico,* pp. 127–28; Orjuela, *Poesías,* pp. 137–318. This poem was found in "Cincuentenario," p. 245, and "Recuerdos," by Arias Argáez, p. 942.

49. McGrady, "Diez Poesías Olvidadas," pp. 62–63; Orjuela, *Poesías,* p. 144. This poem was published in *El Liberal,* Trimester 1, No. 2, Apr. 29, 1884, p. 14.

50. Osiek, *Estudio Estilístico,* p. 134; Orjuela, *Poesías,* p. 145.

51. Ibid. Both this stanza or poem and the one discussed previously were included in an article by Roberto Liévano, "José Asunción Silva," *Revista Chilena,* Santiago, Chile, July 1922, p. 296.

52. Osiek, *Estudio Estilístico,* p. 130; McGrady, "Diez Poesías Olvidadas," p. 57; Orjuela, *Poesías,* pp. 133–34. This poem was published in *Universidad,* Bogotá, No. 106, Nov. 8, 1928, p. 538.

53. *La Lira Nueva,* ed. José María Rivas Groot (Bogotá, 1886), pp. 373–74.

54. Alfredo A. Roggiano, "José Asunción Silva: Aspectos de su Vida y de su Obra," *Cuadernos Hispanoamericanos,* Madrid, No. 9, May–June 1949, p. 597.

55. Osiek, *Estudio Estilístico,* pp. 134–35; Orjuela, *Poesías,* p. 145. This poem was found in "Cincuentenario," p. 251, and "Recuerdos," p. 949, by Arias Argáez.

56. Orjuela, *Poesías,* pp. 152–54. Professor Orjuela says he is using the version given by Osiek, *Estudio Estilístico,* pp. 123–24. Even though the critics accept this poem as one of Silva's, it has rarely been included in the editions of his works. It was found by this author in Roberto Liévano, "Silva and Darío," *Cromos,* Bogotá, May 24, 1924, p. 363; also in Eduardo Carreño, "Silva contra Darío," *Revista Nacional de Cultura,* Caracas, No. 26, March–Apr. 1941, pp. 112–13, reprinted in *Ariel,* San José, Costa Rica, Vol. 43, June 1, 1941, p. 2303. It appeared also in Carlos García Prada, "Silva contra Darío," *Hispania,* Vol. 43, No. 2, May 1960, pp. 176–83, and in the second edition of the biography of Silva by Miramón, pp. 180–83. Liévano and Carreño both testify that the poem was written by Silva although signed with the pseudonym Benjamín Bibelot Ramírez. This poem has been included in at least two editions before its appearance in the Cosmos edition. For example, in *Poesías Completas y sus Mejores Páginas en Prosa,* 1st ed. (Buenos Aires, 1944), pp. 125–26;

on the same pages in the 2nd ed., dated 1945; also in *Poesías Completas*, 4th ed. (Buenos Aires, 1950), pp. 124–25.

57. Orjuela, *Poesías*, p. 127. This poem appeared in *Revista Ilustrada*, Bogotá, Year 1, Vol. 1, No. 3, Aug. 1898, p. 46.

58. Osiek, *Estudio Estilístico*, p. 135; Orjuela, *Poesías*, p. 154. This poem appears in the articles by Arias Argáez, "Cincuentenario," p. 256, and "Recuerdos," p. 950. According to Arias Argáez this poem, which was found in the archives of Arturo Malo O'Leary, was written during a short period of religious fervor which took place in the last years of Silva's life.

59. Pierre Jean Béranger, "Las Golondrinas," translated by José Asunción Silva, *Papel Periódico Ilustrado*, Bogotá, Vol. 2, No. 31, Dec. 16, 1882, p. 108.

60. Pierre Jean Béranger, "Les Hirondelles," *Oeuvres*, New Ed., Vol. 2, *Les Dix Chansons Publiée en 1847* (Paris, 1850), pp. 79–80.

61. Maurice de Guérin, "Imitación," translated by José Asunción Silva, *Papel Periódico Ilustrado*, Bogotá, Vol. 3, No. 50, August 20, 1883, p. 28.

62. Maurice de Guérin, "Fragment," in *Oeuvres*, Vol. 1 (Paris, 1930), p. 59.

63. *Ibid.*

64. In the edition prepared by Orjuela, *Poesías*, p. 126, unfortunately the "cima" (crest) has become by printer's error "cama" (bed), which distorts the whole idea of the poem.

65. Victor Hugo, "Realidad," translated by José Asunción Silva, *Papel Periódico Ilustrado*, Bogotá, Vol. 4, July 24, 1885, p. 370; Orjuela, *Poesías*, pp. 107–108.

66. Victor Hugo, "Réalitè," *Oeuvres Complètes*, Vol. 23, *Les Chansons des Rues et des Bois, Anneés Funestes, L'Ane, La Pitié Suprème* (Paris, 1968), pp. 35–36.

67. "Las Voces Silenciosas," translated by Silva from Alfred Lord Tennyson, appeared in the first edition of the poetry of Silva, entitled there: "De Lord Tennyson," *Poesías* (Barcelona, 1908), pp. 87–91.

68. "The Silent Voices," in *The Works of Alfred Lord Tennyson*, Vol. 8 (London, 1899), p. 280.

Chapter Four

1. Miramón, p. 161.

2. *De Sobremesa, 1887–1896*, 1st ed. (Bogotá, 1925).

3. *De Sobremesa, 1887–1896*, 2nd ed. (Bogotá, [1928]).

4. *Obras Completas* (Bogotá, 1965), pp. 123–310.

5. The author of this work is using the 1928 edition of *De Sobremesa*, listed in note 3. Any citations following this note will be referring to that edition. Notes will not usually be given while summarizing the plot since the elements will be chronological, giving the reader little difficulty in finding the pages.

6. *De Sobremesa*, p. 7.

7. Ibid., p. 15.

8. Ibid., p. 21.

9. The first German edition, *Antertung*, was published in 1893. The two-volume *Dégénéréscence* was translated from the German by Auguste Dietrich (Paris, 1894). Only in 1902 was the work translated into Spanish, by Nicolás Salmerón, *Degeneración* (Madrid, 1902).

10. The first edition, according to *La Grande Encyclopédie*, was published in Paris by her family, *Journal de Marie Bashkirtseff avec Portrait*, 2 vol., 1887.

11. Marie Bashkirtseff, *Journal*, Vol. 2 (Paris, 1914), p. 591.

12. Ibid., Vols. 1 and 2.

13. Max Nordau, *Dégénéréscence*, 2 Vol., translated from the German by Auguste Dietrich (Paris, 1894).

14. *De Sobremesa*, p. 28.

15. "La Legende d'une Cosmopolite," in "Trois Stations de Psychotérapie," *L'Oeuvre de Maurice Barrès*, Vol. 2 (Paris, 1965), pp. 357–68.

16. *De Sobremesa*, p. 50.

17. Ibid., p. 57.

18. Ibid., p. 63 ff.

19. Ibid., p. 74.

20. Ibid., p. 159.

21. Ibid., p. 129.

22. Ibid., p. 177. Daniel Arias Argáez in "Cincuentenario de la Muerte de José Asunción Silva," *Registro Municipal*, Bogotá, June 30, 1946, pp. 254–55, cites the long digression and testifies that it belonged to another novel by Silva which was lost in the sinking of the ship *L'Amerique*, and that probably Silva added these lines because of their beauty.

23. Ibid., p. 178.

24. Ibid., p. 183.

25. Ibid., p. 186

26. Ibid., p. 220.

27. Bernardo Gicovate, *Conceptos Fundamentales de Literatura Comparada: Iniciación a la Poesía Modernista* (San Juan, Puerto Rico, 1962), p. 124.

28. Daniel Arias Argáez, "Cincuentenario de la Muerte de José Asunción Silva," *Registro Municipal,* Bogotá, June 30, 1946, pp. 242–65.

29. Juan Loveluck, "*De Sobremesa,* Novela Desconocida del Modernismo," *Revista Iberoamericana,* Vol. 31, No. 59, January–June 1965, p. 25.

30. *De Sobremesa,* p. 46.

31. Ibid., p. 205.

32. Ibid., pp. 21, 183.

33. Ibid., p. 15.

34. Ibid., pp. 64–71.

35. Ibid., p. 133.

36. Ibid., p. 182.

37. Ibid., p. 183.

38. Ibid., pp. 133–34.

39. Ibid., p. 134.

40. Ibid., pp. 104, 172.

41. Ibid., p. 17.

42. Ibid., p. 176.

43. Ibid., p. 21.

44. Juan Evangelista Manrique, "José Asunción Silva: Recuerdos Intimos," *La Revista de América,* Paris, Vol. 6, January 1914, p. 32.

45. *De Sobremesa,* p. 127.

46. Bernardo Gicovate, op. cit. (see above, note 27), p. 124 ff.

47. *Oeuvres Complètes de Joris-Karl Huysmans,* Vol. 7, *A Rebours* (Paris, 1929).

48. *De Sobremesa,* p. 10.

49. Ibid., p. 202.

50. Silva uses this term: "rubendariacos" ("in the manner of Rubén Darío") in a letter to Baldomero Sanín Cano reproduced in José Asunción Silva, *Obras Completas* (Bogotá, 1965), p. 378.

Chapter Five

1. José Asunción Silva, "La Protesta de la Musa," *Revista Literaria,* Bogotá, Vol. 2, December 14, 1890, pp. 133–35.

2. José Asunción Silva, "Al Carbon," *Obras Completas* (Bogotá, 1965), pp. 317–18.

3. José Asunción Silva, "Al Pastel," *Obras Completas,* pp. 318–19.

4. José Asunción Silva, "Suspiros," *Obras Completas,* pp. 319–21.

5. Emilio Cuervo Márquez, "José Asunción Silva," in *Ensayos y Conferencias* (Bogotá, 1937), pp. 212–13.

6. José Asunción Silva, "El Paraguas del Padre León," *Obras Completas*, pp. 326–29.

7. Donald McGrady discovered this narration in the *Sunday Supplement* of *El Espectador*, May 27, 1951. He discusses the plot, and the possibility that it may be an original story by Silva, in his article: "Un Cuento Atribuido a Silva," *Thesaurus: Boletín del Instituto Caro y Cuervo*, Vol. 24, No. 2, May–August 1971, p. 347.

8. Ibid., pp. 350–54.

9. José Asunción Silva, "El Doctor Rafael Núñez," *Obras Completas*, pp. 330–35. The first publication of this article was with the same title, in *El Cojo Ilustrado*, Caracas, Vol. 3, No. 67, December 1, 1894, pp. 379–80.

10. José Asunción Silva, "El Doctor Rafael Núñez," *Obras Completas*, pp. 330–35.

11. José Asunción Silva, "Prologo al Poema 'Bienaventurados los que Lloran,'" *Obras Completas*, p. 323.

12. Ibid., p. 326.

13. José Asunción Silva, "Pierre Loti," *Obras Completas*, pp. 341–42.

14. José Asunción Silva, "El Cofre de Nacar," "Noticia Bibliografica y Literaria [sobre Anatole France]," *Obras Completas*, p. 336.

15. Ibid., pp. 336–40. The same essay which was discussed was published under the title "Anatole France," in *Cosmópolis*, Caracas, Vol. 2, No. 9, October 31, 1894, pp. 125–28.

16. José Asunción Silva, "El Conde León Tolstoi," *Obras Completas*, 1965, pp. 343–45.

17. José Asunción Silva, "Letter to the Editor," in *El Telegrama del Domingo, 1888*, reproduced and entitled "Critica Ligera," in *Antología de Verso y Prosa*, Bogotá, Instituto Colombiano de Cultura (Biblioteca Colombiana de Cultura, Colección Popular, 82), 1972, pp. 73–81.

18. The most plausible date for this letter which can be established by the author of this book is sometime in 1892, since in the letter Silva says that his visit to the Señora was two years ago, and Daniel Arias Argáez attests in "Cincuentenario de la Muerte de José Asunción Silva," *Registro Municipal*, Bogotá, June 30, 1946, p. 257, that the visit was shortly after the publication of "La Protesta de la Musa," December 14, 1890, op. cit. (see note 1 above).

19. José Asunción Silva, *Prosas y Versos*, ed. Carlos García Prada, 2nd ed. (Madrid, 1960), p. 58.

20. Ibid.

21. Ibid., p. 59.

22. From *Imitation of Christ*, Book 2, Chapter 10, attributed to Thomas à Kempis, German mystic (1379–1471).

23. *Biblioteca Popular: Colección de Grandes Escritores*, Vol. 2 (Bogotá, 1893), pp. 1–31.

24. "La Misa de las Sombras," in *Biblioteca Popular: Colección de Grandes Escritores*, Vol. 2 (Bogotá, 1893), p. 4.

25. "La Messe des Ombres," in Anatole France, *L'Etui de Nacre* (Paris, n.d.), p. 5.

26. "Baltasar," in *Biblioteca Popular: Colección de Grandes Escritores*, Vol. 2 (Bogotá, 1893), p. 23.

27. Anatole France, "Baltasar," in *Baltasar* (Paris, n.d.), p. 17.

28. Daniel Arias Argáez, "Cincuentenario de la Muerte de José Asunción Silva," *Registro Municipal*, Bogotá, June 30, 1946, p. 247.

29. Donald McGrady, "Un Cuento Atribuido a Silva," in *Thesaurus: Boletín del Instituto Caro y Cuervo*, Vol. 27, No. 2, May–August 1971, pp. 347–54.

Chapter Six

1. José Asunción Silva, *Poesías* (Barcelona, 1908).

2. Miguel de Unamuno y Jugo, "Prólogo," in *Poesías* (Barcelona, 1908).

3. Juan Ramón Jiménez, *Españoles de Tres Mundos* (Buenos Aires, 1942), p. 55.

4. *De Sobremesa, 1887–1896*, 1st ed. (Bogotá, 1925).

Selected Bibliography

The Bibliography below includes in the "Primary Sources" only those editions which are felt to be the most authoritative. The "Secondary Sources" include the basic works which have been consulted, as well as others considered to be essential references for the researcher. For more complete listings the reader should consult the bibliographies listed under "Secondary Sources."

PRIMARY SOURCES

1. Editions of Works

Poesías. Prologue by Miguel de Unamuno. Barcelona: Imprenta de Pedro Ortega, Casa Editorial Maucci, 1908.

Poesías. Definitive Edition. Prologue by Miguel de Unamuno and Chile: Condor, 1923.

Poesías. Definitive Edition. Prolouge by Miguel de Unamuno and Notes by Baldomero Sanín Cano. Paris: Michaud, 1923.

De Sobremesa, 1887–1896. 1st ed., Bogotá: Cromos, 1925; 2nd ed., [1928].

El Libro de Versos, 1883–1896. Bogotá: Cromos, [1928].

Poesías Completas. Buenos Aires: Sopena, 1st ed., 1941; 2nd ed., 1943; 3rd ed., 1945; 4th ed., 1950.

Prosas y Versos. Introduction, Selection, and Notes by Carlos García Prada. Mexico City: Editorial Cultura, 1942; 2nd ed., Madrid: Ediciones Iberoamericanas, 1960.

Poesías Completas y sus Mejores Páginas en Prosa. Prologue by Arturo Capdevila. 1st ed., Buenos Aires: Elevación, 1944.

Poesías. Selection and Prologue by Francisca Chica Salas. Buenos Aires: Estrada, 1945.

El Libro de Versos. Facsimile edition of the manuscript written by Silva, without pagination. Bogotá: Editorial Horizonte, 1945.

El Libro de Versos. Publicaciones del Ministerio de Educación de Colombia. Bogotá: Prensas de la Biblioteca Nacional, 1946.

Poésias Completas Seguidas de Prosas Selectas. Biographical Note by Camilo de Brigard Silva. Prologue by Miguel de Unamuno. Madrid: Aguilar, 1st ed., 1951; 2nd ed., 1952; 3rd ed., 1963.

El Libro de Versos y Otras Poesías. Madrid: Ediciones Guadarrama, 1954.

Obra Completa (Prosa y Verso). Prologue by Rafael Maya. Biblioteca de Autores Colombianos. Ministerio de Educación Nacional. Bogotá: Ediciones de la Revista Bolívar, 1956.

Obras Completas. Bogotá: Banco de la República, 1965.

Obras Completas. 2 vols. Buenos Aires: Plus Ultra, 1968.

Obra Completa de José Asunción Silva. Medellín: Editorial Bedout, 1970.

Poesías. Edition, Introduction, and Notes by Hector H. Orjuela. Biblioteca "Colombia Literaria." Bogotá: Cromos, 1973.

Intimidades, Edición, Prólogo y Estudio Preliminar por Hector H. Orjuela, Serie "La Granada Entreabierta," 18, Bogotá: Instituto Caro y Cuervo, 1977.

SECONDARY SOURCES

1. Selected Bibliographies

ANDERSON, ROBERT ROLAND. "José Asunción Silva (1865–1896)," in *Spanish-American Modernism: A Selected Bibliography.* Tucson, Arizona: The University of Arizona Press, 1970, pp. 144–48. Contains 125 of the more valuable secondary sources. Rigorous accuracy in data.

OSIEK, BETTY TYREE. "Bibliografía," in *José Asuncíon Silva: Estudio Estilístico de su Poesía.* Mexico City: Ediciones de Andrea, 1968, pp. 186–204. Not a selective bibliography. Lists 205 studies on Silva, some general studies on Modernism, 35 editions of Silva's works, and the date of first publication of the poems and essays which came out during his life, as well as the first publication date of many of the other compositions, prose, and poetry after his death.

2. Books

CAPARROSO, ARTURO. *Silva.* 2nd ed., Buenos Aires: Gráficas Ellacuria, 1954. Discusses Silva's literary home and resulting love of letters. Skillfully analyzes selected poems on childhood themes, ironic poetry, the "Nocturno," *De Sobremesa,* and other prose. Considers that Fernández was Silva's alter ego. Is convinced that although decadent, Silva fell short of being a Symbolist.

CUERVO MÁRQUEZ, EMILIO. "José Asunción Silva: Su Vida y su Obra," in *Ensayos y Conferencias.* Bogotá: Cromos, 1937, pp. 190–229;

earlier in book form with the same title, Amsterdam: Editorial "De Faam," 1925. Life of Silva examined by a contemporary who describes traditional Bogotá and the reactions to first French literary influences. Feels Silva returned from France with new and optimistic ideas about his brilliant literary future. Judges that Silva suffered from various quirks and idiosyncrasies, and lacked sufficient friends to support him in difficult times. Wisely, gives no credit to incest legend. Believed that Silva accommodated his poems to the rhythm of his life.

GHIANO, JUAN CARLOS. *José Asunción Silva*. Enciclopedia Literaria 16, España e Hispanoamérica. Buenos Aires: Centro Editor de América Latina, 1967. Brief biographical précis followed by a panoramic view of Silva's production. Evaluates his contributions to Spanish-American literature and his influence on later generations. Minimal selected bibliography and chronology terminates the work.

LIÉVANO, ROBERTO. *En Torno a Silva: Selección de Estudios e Investigaciones sobre la Obra y la Vida Intima del Poeta*. Bogotá: Editorial El Gráfico, 1946. In poetic style examines Silva's life of physical and spiritual elegance, soon marred by tragedies. Considers that Silva was tormented by doubts, but was able to express them in poems of deep emotion and lasting beauty. Denies categorically the suspicion of incest; attests that Silva had various love affairs. Agrees that he is a consummate Modernist, as well as interpreter of his native ambience. Peruses his commercial letters and marvels at his perseverance in spite of repeated failure. Posits mutual influence of Silva and Darío, concluding that Silva preceded Darío.

MIRAMÓN, ALBERTO. *José Asunción Silva: Ensayo Biogáfico con Documentos Inéditos*. 1st ed., Bogotá: Imprenta Nacional, 1937; 2nd ed., Bogotá: Litografía Villegas, 1957. The second edition has the addition of four letters written by Silva to Rufino J. Cuervo, and an article by Luis de Zulueta entitled: "Silva Visto desde España." Indispensable biography of the Modernist writer.

OSIEK, BETTY TYREE. *José Asunción Silva: Estudio Estilístico de su Poesía*. Mexico City: Ediciones de Andrea, 1968. A study of the style of Silva's poetry based on a vocabulary count and concordance to discover predominant themes and motifs for analysis. Contains section on stylistic techniques and syntactic structures, as well as one on his rhythm, rhyme, and meter. (See Section 1 of "Secondary Sources" above for bibliographical information on this book.)

3. Periodical Articles and Essays in Books (Only Selected Items Are Included Here)

ARIAS, ALEJANDRO C. "José Asunción Silva," in *Ensayos: Goethe, José Asunción Silva, Stefan Zweig.* Salto, Uruguay: Tipografía Mazzara, 1936, pp. 89–100. Defines personality of Silva as aristocratic, superrefined. Analysis of several poems including the "Nocturno," "Gotas Amargas," and others of ironic inspiration. Believes that the neuroticism of Silva led him to an incestuous passion for his sister Elvira.

ARIAS ARGÁEZ, DANIEL. "Cincuentenario de la Muerte de José Asunción Silva," *Registro Municipal,* Bogotá, June 30, 1946, pp. 242–65.

————. "Recuerdos de José Asunción Silva," *Bolivar,* Bogotá, Vol. 5, Nov.-Dec. 1951, pp. 939–64. Contemporary of Silva. Gives some unknown poems and presents the proof that some attributed to Silva were by others. Discusses some of his personal memories of Silva and of his disequilibrium with his surroundings. Elucidates several things which happened in Silva's lifetime. Describes his final tragic years ending in suicide, and discusses his last poem dedicated to Bolívar.

BAR-LEWAW, ITZHAK, "José Asunción Silva: Apuntes sobre su Obra," in *Temas Literarios Iberoamericanos.* Mexico City: B. Costa-Amic, 1961, pp. 47–77. Judges it necessary to know the life, ambience, hereditary factors to understand the doubting poet. Obsessed with death and other melancholy themes, as were Poe and Bécquer. Analyzes his translations of poems and terminates by deliberating upon Silva as an outstanding Modernist writer.

BOTERO, EBEL. "José A. Silva," in *Cinco Poetas Colombianos: Estudios sobre Silva, Valencia, Luis Carlos Lopez, Rivera y Maya.* Manizales: Imprenta Departmental, 1964, pp. 15–40. Unorthodox and controversial critic rigorously scrutinizes dates of birth and death of Silva. Justly criticizes Miramón's biography as lyrical and unorganized. Discounts the idea that Silva had no childhood. Considers that he was timid but had a normal sex life. Analyzes his atheism, and considers that he had an exceptional scientific mind. Catalogues critics' ideas concerning his literary placement and feels he reflects his native country. Denies Poe is main influence.

GARCÍA PRADA, CARLOS. "Introducción," in *José Asunción Silva. Prosas y Versos.* Mexico City: Cultura, 1942, ix–xxxv; also in 2nd ed., Madrid: Ediciones Iberoamericanas, 1960, pp. 7–42. Biographical résumé considering his surroundings and the unfortunate events of his life as they affected Silva. Subjects selected poems by Silva to examination and concludes that his work is Modernist with some Romantic traces.

GICOVATE, BERNARDO. "José Asunción Silva y la Decadencia Europea," in *Conceptos Fundamentales de Literatura Comparada: Iniciación de la Poesía Modernista*. San Juan, Puerto Rico: Ediciones Asomante, 1962, pp. 117–38. Conceives of Silva as one of the best poets of his epoch, original and with few obvious influences because of prodigious absorption powers. Excellent analysis of themes and techniques of novel and various poems, elucidating such tendencies as decadence and symbolism.

HENRÍQUEZ UREÑA, MAX. "José Asunción Silva," in *Breve Historia del Modernismo*. 2nd ed., Mexico City: Fondo de Cultura Económica, 1962, pp. 135–37. Beginning with "Nocturno's" appearance in 1894 explores Silva's burgeoning influence. Considers most important poems, mentioning similarities with Bartrina in "Gotas Amargas," and gives credence to Poe's influence on Silva. Reviews life and happenings which led to suicide. Concludes that Silva's end-of-century pessimism is unique in poetry in the Spanish language.

LOVELUCK, JUAN, "*De Sobremesa*, Novela Desconocida del Modernismo," *Revista Iberoamericana*, Vol. 31, No. 59, Jan.-June 1965, pp. 17–32. Effort to create awareness of Modernist prose. Investigates aspects of Modernist novel *De Sobremesa*, which, like the French novels of those years, preferred a neuropathic hero. Describes intellectual surroundings of Silva and the effect of the tragic loss of manuscripts. Elucidates anguished, end-of-century, aristocratic attitudes in the novel. Demonstrates Silva's use of fusion of painting and poetry to reflect scenes.

MANCINI, GUIDO. "Notas Marginales a las Poesías de José Asunción Silva," in *Thesaurus: Boletín del Instituto Caro y Cuervo*, Bogotá, Vol. 16, No. 3, Sept.-Dec. 1961, pp. 614–38. Masterful exegesis of selected poems concentrating on his pain-provoking pessimism and his musicality, plus some favorite themes, as death and the poetic art. Postulates Silva's love of life with an unresigned pessimism resulting from disillusionment. Denies a strong Becquerian influence, demonstrating that he was Modernist and Symbolist.

MANRIQUE, JUAN EVANGELISTA. "José Asunción Silva: (Recuerdos Intimos)." *La Revista de América*. Paris, Vol. 6, Jan. 1914, pp. 28–41. Communicates memories of the privileges of his friend Silva in childhood and adolescence. Describes their relations during Silva's visit to Paris, characterizing his avid search for knowledge. Considers that he was neurasthenic in his reactions to misfortunes. Explains famous heart-marking episode.

MAYA, RAFAEL. "José Asunción Silva," *De Silva a Rivera* (*Elogios*). Bogotá: Publicaciones de la Revista "Universidad," 1929, pp. 3–25. Characterizes Silva as pantheist preoccupied with perpetual change, anguished intellectually but not morally. Explores his principal themes, such as the reconquering of lost time. Opines that he was an end-of-century writer who took refuge in the aesthetic past. Judges he was Symbolist and pure poet, but also Romantic *sui generis* with Modernist tendencies. Suffered the tragic consequences of being an intellectual in a shallow ambience.

ORJUELA, HECTOR H. "Estudio preliminar," in *Intimidades*, Serie "La Granada Entreabierta," 18, Bogotá: Instituto Caro y Cuervo, 1977, pp. 1–42. A discussion of his acquisition precedes the initial publication of twenty-seven original poems and six translations from a copy of a notebook of adolescent poems by Silva. Orjuela explains also his inclusion of twenty-six previously published but not widely known poems from that same notebook, and others from recondite periodicals, most of which were examined earlier by Donald McGrady, Hector Orjuela, or Betty Tyree Osiek. Documents how he obtained this copy which is in the handwriting of a feminine friend of Silva. Analyzes these early poems, concluding that although they are the least important artistically, it was necessary that they be published in the interests of completeness.

ORJUELA, HECTOR H. "La Primera Versión del 'Nocturno' de Silva," *Thesaurus: Boletín del Instituto Caro y Cuervo*. Vol. 29, No. 1, Jan.-Apr. 1974, pp. 118–28. Discloses the process by which he found, after eighty years, when all other investigators had failed, the location of the first publication of the famous "Nocturno." Compares the first version which he discovered with the succeeding version.

ROGGIANO, ALFREDO A. "José Asunción Silva: Aspectos de su Vida y de su Obra," *Cuadernos Hispanoamericanos*. Madrid, No. 9, May-June 1949, pp. 593–612. Clarifies some aspects of Silva's biography and exhibits the essential problem of a hypersensitive artist in a materialistic world with a disappointing reality. Ably subjects to examination influences of other poets, and explicates the favorite themes of Silva. Concludes with an analysis of the most typical poems which express Silva's Modernism.

SANÍN CANO, BALDOMERO. "En el Cincuentenario del Poeta José Asunción Silva," *Revista de las Indias*. Bogotá, Vol. 28, No. 89,

May 1946, pp. 161–78. An intelligent and perceptive critic and also Silva's personal friend, Sanín Cano deliberates upon Silva's personality, knowledge, and poetic art. Considers that his failures, torments, and pessimism were accentuated because of being born in an unpropitious time.

UNAMUNO, MIGUEL DE. "José Asunción Silva," in *Poesías*. Barcelona: Imprenta de Pedro Ortega, Casa Editorial Maucci, 1908. (This is the only article Unamuno did for an edition of the works of Silva and it is often reproduced with the date of 1918. It appears with the date 1918 in the edition of the Banco de la República with the exact text as in the 1908 edition.) After reading only forty-five of Silva's poems in an expurgated edition, Unamuno analyzes the poet superficially because of seeing his poetic art narrowly. He judges correctly that he loved childhood and was obsessed with death, but incorrectly in attributing a puerile and sentimental unity of the two. He attests that Silva committed suicide because he could no longer be a child. Errs in attributing to Silva only a chaste and pure spiritualized love. His biographical information was erroneous; however, one can say that his poetic prologue greatly augmented Silva's fame in spite of his misinterpretations and inaccuracies.

VALENCIA, GUILLERMO. "José Asunción Silva," *Nosotros*, Buenos Aires, Year 3, Vol. 4, 1909, pp. 162–76. The same article was published in various periodicals criticizing the first edition of *Poesías*, including the prologue by Unamuno. Believes his adolescent poems are not important enough to be included. Is extremely critical of Unamuno's misjudgment of the Colombian. Discusses Silva's rebellion and reactionary attitude toward society as reflected in ironic poems and in "Gotas Amargas."

Index